MW01644244

A Madman's Gospel

A DISPLAY OF CHRIST IN OUR MODERN WORLD

JAY T. ATTEBERY AACS, BSTM, MNCM, MISM

WestBow Press books may be ordered through booksellers or by contacting:

WestBow Press
A Division of Thomas Nelson & Zondervan
1663 Liberty Drive
Bloomington, IN 47403
www.westbowpress.com
844-714-3454

ISBN: 979-8-3850-4119-0 (sc)
ISBN: 979-8-3850-4120-6 (hc)
ISBN: 979-8-3850-4121-3 (e)

Library of Congress Control Number: 2024927249

Print information available on the last page.

WestBow Press rev. date: 02/06/2025

CONTENTS

ACKNOWLEDGMENTS

I would like to thank Jesus Christ for all that he has done for me. He has done for me what I could not do for myself in my powerless and inadequate human state. He interceded to save my life beyond my wildest expectations and what I deserved. The arrangement Christ made with me was simple and effective, for he has kept his word, as I have kept mine. He has made provisions in every event along the way in my life's journey. These provisions were the things I needed and the guidance to lead me where I needed to be. He has always provided a means of escape and the peace to take the alternative of his word. I thank him for teaching me the requirements needed for repentance, change, and growth while putting them into practical use along with intimate interaction with him. I am grateful for Christ's interactive intercession that has been totally reliable and unmerited. I cannot give him enough praise for his consistency and faithfulness in my life.

I wrote this book for the love of my life, Fern. I got tired of people from other religious systems questioning my faith, attempting to create doubt. Because of their constant demands to prove my faith to them, this book is the culmination of my fulfillment and reason for my faith in Christ. Isaiah 1:18 (NKJV) tells us, "Come now, and let us reason together," but the Christian Standard Bible states, "Come let us settle this," and the defense of my faith is what this book is all about. This then is what I have come to understand in belief after thirty-five attempts to qualify my faith to others.

I thank my son David. He is deaf and blind, and he requires my tenacity, integrity, congruency, and unrelenting faith to fight for his needs. He has been a great help to me while writing this. In addition, I love my son Jacob, who frequently questioned me concerning my life before he came along. I hope this will answer a lot of his questions regarding my being a prodigal son. The status I once had in my youth and the doctrinal issue I have come to believe in are addressed within the context of these words for him. This is also for my estranged children, as an example of putting my mouth where my heart lives.

In addition, this word of love is for all my unbelieving friends. It was they who challenged me concerning my faith in Christ and the validness of the foundation of that faith. I hope it opens their eyes to see, opens their ears to hear, and touches their hearts in a world of deception, dishonesty, and disqualification of the scriptures.

I thank my friends who are in the fellowship of believers. At my church, they helped me significantly, offered unrelenting critiques, and challenged the readability of my writing style. Over the years, I have had to learn how to write, and this work is the result.

This text has no reference to the concepts of cults. However, it faces all the issues I have had in facing the dishonesty, the deception, the avoidance of the truth, and the consistent heeding of double standards in life surrounded by the misrepresentation. I have attempted to point the way to the foundation of scripture as the validation of my faith. There is no need to hold in contempt all those who have taken the time to condemn me for mine repeatedly. I find no need to belittle those who have done so. Yet I do find the need to put in black and white the credentials of faith in Christ with an honest examination and some direct reasoning. Once again, let me reiterate the Christian Study Bible's rendition, which states, "Come let us settle the issue," which makes sense in the process of validation of the faith that lies within me. Yet when reasoning gets thrown out the window and is no longer viable, it seems a worthless process to discuss issues associated with Christ and his status, authority, redemption, remission of sin, and being the only son of God as the Lamb of God. Reason is a serious concern in understanding not just the scriptures but the purpose of salvation through Jesus Christ.

However, for me, this work settles the issue of any doubt concerning my faith in Christ. It settles the validity of God's word, Christ's authority, the singularity of the Father of heaven as God, and that there is no other. Jesus is the author and finisher of my faith. He has given to me the remission and atonement of sin through the shedding of his blood on the cross of Calvary.

Thus, one can take my words here as my witness of Jesus. However, there are things to do within this work for both the believer and nonbeliever alike. It will be confrontive of the doctrines I hold. It will be an in-your-face style of writing with the issue of Christ being himself, as he was, is, and will be to come. This work is an act of love to set the path straight, validate the reasoning for the path, and establish the foundation of an unshakeable faith in Christ.

INTRODUCTION

There is a rule in Critical Thinking that suggests this: when an argument is founded upon a false premise, no matter what follows, whether true or false, the argument is considered valid.

The above quote first came to me in a class on critical thinking. The argument I had with the Harvard professor at the junior college was intense, as I contended that this concept was invalid and propagating a lie. The professor, however, taught and considered the concept a valid one. Our discussion became heated. Of course, the underlying issue with this critical thinking argument is that it is considered a valid argument. Yet because this argument is upheld as valid, many people believe that it must be true.

However, many people are at odds with this concept. When they hear it for the first time, the thought of this fallacy argument's concept being valid really gets them worked up. The concept of a lie being valid is appalling, and to accept a fallacy, a lie, as an accurate or valid statement is even worse. Even in the circle of unbelievers, they stand in disbelief when it comes to this argument. Yet this concept used in everyday life causes us to face misunderstandings, such as the misrepresentation of doctrine and even the exploitations of the faith. It is even harder to accept a lie as the truth or, worse, as a valid concept when living an honest life with integrity. Believers dismayed with the frustration born from this concept find this type of communication belittling because of its futile deception. Beyond this, when the masses accept it and it is validated by others, any confrontation or contention becomes pointless. The point is that we accept this concept in our dealings in everyday living. It has the appearance of a lack of integrity in the communication between people, religion systems, and even sects of people. People in many chosen religious systems still accept it as an honorable spiritual belief that they follow in the form of spiritual life.

However, there is only one exception to this rule: The lie-based argument must be accepted, and that must be followed by the submissive acceptance of the false and true statements. These submitted arguments accepted as valid truth are then used in everyday life as core spiritual beliefs. In fact, these are the hardest of places to look for falsehoods in doctrines, for they are found in our own personhood as accepted beliefs. If you follow a false belief after having accepted it, the immense amount of frustration, the crushing disbelief, and the shame of later renouncing it are more than most people can face or even consider facing. Therefore, this crushing blow to faith becomes the landmark that most will not cross to meet Jesus on his terms. This Christ, this Son of God in the flesh dwelling among us, is quoted in Matthew's writing: "Let your word be, yes, yes; no, no. For whatever is more than these comes from evil."[1]

Thus, there seems to be a fallacy argument about Jesus that stems from an evil statement of belief. Yet this fallacy argument influences the morality, integrity, and actions of a great many good religious people in our world today. And in this way, false belief becomes valid. Paul discusses this same issue with the Corinthians,[2] that this argument of belief is a matter of its use and presentation. This form of a valid lie-based argument leads to and from dishonesty and deception and is manipulation that ends in judgment. When this misrepresentation of the biblical scriptures occurs, it leads people astray and away from God. The concept of a false premise is always the foundation for misleading people into these deceptions and the acceptance of the lie-based faith. This becomes an unconfronted and unconditional blindness of faith within any religious system of belief. This type of falsified argument requires the combination of both false and true statements, which people accept and condone as valid, accurate, honest, and true. This is the nature of Satan's process for humanity's slavery to sin. Therefore, the examination of the gospel message of Jesus Christ, based on the foundation of the scriptures, is the necessity of the message before us.

The beginning of understanding is the fear of the Lord. The scriptures begin with infusion of the Holy Spirit into one's life. The psalmist, King David, wrote, "Create in me a clean heart, O God, and renew a steadfast spirit with me. Do not cast me away from your presence, and do not take your Holy Spirit from me. Restore in me the joy of your salvation, and uphold me by your generous Spirit."[3] The God-shaped hole everyone experiences is evidence in our real lives of our need for him. All too often, our lack of a quiet mind and a peaceful heart, combined with our own desires, plagues the experience of understanding God, and we miss his provisions for us. David was searching for a new life. He was looking for an alternative through God's Spirit. David knew the power of God's Holy Spirit in his life and the magnitude of his need for restoration. This need for the Holy Spirit as the guide during our search of the scriptures is the interaction with God. It is through them and the personal revelation of Christ in confirmation of that scripture that we develop a respect for God.

Our needs will be confronted. Isaiah, in his confrontation of us concerning our search for God, our status, and the state of our existing condition with God, wrote, "For thus says the High and Lofty One, who inhabits eternity, whose name is Holy: 'I dwell in the high and holy place, with him, who has a contrite and humble spirit, to revive the spirit of the humble and to revive the heart of the contrite ones.'"[4] This status of repentance is the standing condition of our hearts in the contriteness and humility of character toward God. He reacts to this repentance and draws us to himself, and his salvation fills our need. This Holy Spirit teaches us what is required in the confrontation of our faith.[5] This helper, this comforter from Christ, has the job description of conviction of sin, righteousness, and judgment,[6] and here is the reasoning for it:

1. "Sin, because they [the unbeliever] do not believe in Me."
2. "Righteousness, because I go to My Father and you see Me no more."
3. "Judgment, because the ruler of this world is judged."

Consequently, the study of the biblical scripture is a requirement for the believer in Christ. In addition, we need to ask the Holy Spirit to help us in the process of searching the scripture during our interaction with God. Thus, the beginning of any biblical study requires asking the Holy Spirit for guidance. However, the issues in life come from our blindness to our chosen sins, our inadequacies in establishing righteous behavior, and our lack of functional judgment on both sin and righteousness. Furthermore, these conditions stemming from our chosen sins are exacerbated by our acceptance of deception and withdraw us from the presence of God. We accept sin as normal in our lives, and then we call this condoned chosen behavior valid and acceptable. We need something to witness to us, and this witness is the Holy Spirit, who is a direct witness to our condition in life.[7] In addition to the Holy Spirit, the second witness is the black-and-white confirmation of the scripture in our faces concerning those chosen sins. Therefore, three witnesses come forward to influence us: "For there are three that bear witness in heaven: The Father, the Word, and the Holy Spirit, and these three are one [in unity]."[8] So we need to request the help of the Holy Spirit as we examine biblical scripture, exposing the state of our existence and condition of our lives, requiring the alignment of our lives with God's holiness through the scripture, and being a witness of Jesus Christ.

However, so many times, we do not ask for actual help from the Holy Spirit. At first, we look for relief from our own shame, guilt, and fear, wanting to have peace in our lives through association with any god of any sort (any created idolatry in replacement of God, that is). Jesus Christ is our actual help. As our great High Priest, he is always making intercession for us. Therefore, many of our prayers need to ask for peace in our hearts and quietness in our minds. It might sound like this, if you dare to say this prayer aloud:

Dear Holy Spirit,

I ask you to guide me during my reading and study of the scripture. I ask you to help me to avoid the wickedness and weaknesses of my own heart. I ask you to open my eyes to see so I can glean the knowledge of lifting Christ up and apply scripture in my life. I ask you to open my ears to hear so I can understand the wisdom of your written word in appropriate, discernable implementation into my life. I ask you to soften my heart for the implantation of the scripture into a contrite and humble life and grow what I need to become closer to my Father in heaven.

I ask you to be a revealer in my life. I ask you to expose the sin in my life so I can begin to clear my heart of the obstacles between the Father of heaven and me through repentance. I ask you to educate me in righteousness so I can live a life of consistent unity with Christ. I ask to be of use, effectively enabled for his purposes and service. I ask you to judge me according to your word so I may have a clean heart before you. I ask you to lead me to Christ for the remission of my sins, and I ask you to lead me to the exposure of my secret sins, concerning what I have not seen, through daily repentance. I need your guidance to make honest and rightful decisions on what I need in my life and in my future with you, as well. I ask for wisdom to do that which is set before me to accomplish in life in active worship and honor of Christ. I ask for understanding of your word as I study its content.

I ask you to do this in the name of Jesus, Amen.

CHAPTER 1

SATAN'S MANIFESTO

How you are fallen from heaven, O Lucifer, son of the morning! How you are cut down to the ground, you who weakened the nations! For you have said in your heart: "I will ascend into heaven, I will exalt my throne above the stars of God; I will also sit on the mount of the congregation on the farthest sides of the north; I will ascend above the clouds, I will be like the Most High." Yet, you shall be brought down to Sheol, to the lowest depths of the pit.[9]

Satan's ultimate aim has always been to take God's place. That is, we put blinders on toward God, spit in his face, kick him to the curb as useless, and take his place as God in our lives. Isaiah wrote of Satan's manifesto, describing it as having the foundation of pride. Lucifer wanted exaltation above God's throne,[10] entrusted with the authority to control and speak the governing law to us and to Jesus Christ, who is the Jehovah Elohiym[11] (Lord God). Satan, this son of the morning's standard, desires to be God's equal in life, and although Christ is the first and last,[12] Satan is looking to usurp this king of Israel, this Christ, this Jehovah.[13] For Jesus Christ is God and there is no other.[14] Satan can never take Christ's place in the lives of humans; he can only manipulate them with his deception by overcoming them with his misrepresentations of Jesus.

Although Job was not alive at the time of Christ, he understood the resurrection knowledge of Christ. For Job writes, "I know my

Redeemer lives.... I shall see God.... [M]y eyes shall behold, and not another. How my heart yearns within me."[15] It is foolish to attempt to make anything equal to Christ[16] because, when it concerns knowing God, these people, who do "not glorify Him as God, neither [are] ... thankful ... [but] become vain in their imaginations and their foolish heart,[17]" become darkened. Satan's desire is to usurp God's authority and take his place, promoting and flaunting his equality in front of his creation.

Satan takes advantage of us as easy prey. In the beginning, when God created Adam and made Eve as his helpmate, their relationship with Jehovah Elohiym was the only real relationship they had. This Jehovah Elohiym is Jesus Christ, the creator of all things. They walked with him in innocence during the cool of the day. They communicated with him face to face, as an ongoing normal activity of relating with Jesus daily. The search for easy prey on which to impose the most damage in God's world is Satan's standard of conduct.

Adam and Eve were as innocent children. Like children in a bathtub, playing and splashing about without knowledge of their condition or status was normal for them. Adam was not a priest of the Jehovah Elohiym (called the Most High God), nor did he require one. These two children of God's creation had a relationship with this righteous, holy, pure, and eternal God. This relationship was face to face with him. This face-to-face relationship was like an intimate family having a conversation with Christ. This was Adam and Eve's normal daily existence. There was no need for a priest or priesthood until the intrusion and corruption of sin that came into their lives because of Adam. There was no requirement or need for the Aaronic or Melchizedekian priesthood until after this corruption of Eve and the sin of Adam. The sin of Adam came from going against God's command of him not to eat of the fruit of the tree of knowledge of good and evil. The corruption of Eve was believing that she could be like God himself. Thus, the most damage created in God's creation was the deception imposed upon Eve that led to Adam's decision to sin in disobedience to the relationship and authority of Christ.

Satan used persuasive words to deceive Eve. This deception affected Adam's decision to eat the fruit of the tree. In his letter to the Colossians, Paul warns us against the deception of persuasive words.[18] Satan used persuasive words to bring about Eve's corruption in the garden, and he uses the same technique repeatedly upon us today. First, Satan uses isolation to separate people from their healthy support. This gets people away from the foundation of scripture, from their supportive staff, as well as from their healthy peers and creates doubt in the safety and security of their faith. Eve was the first prey exposed to Satan's force of persuasion, isolating her from God and Adam.

We can see this in the reeducation of Eve by Lucifer's words of seduction. This seduction happens when Satan confronts her with the issue of eating from all the trees of the garden.[19] Her compliant response to this serpent of old acknowledged that she knew she was to "not eat, nor shall you touch it, lest you die."[20] Adam, charged with the tending and caring for the garden, now has included Eve. However, Eve expresses a misunderstanding of this statement. She added the condition of "nor shall you touch it" to Christ's command to Adam, misrepresenting that command. Satan begins his plan against God through the craftiness of his words to deceive her by using her own misrepresentations of God's command. Now, Satan uses this misrepresentation with us regarding the value of God's word to us, our actions toward him, and the faith required for salvation.

It is the nature of innocent children to protect one another from the possibility of harm. Adam does this for Eve by trying to keep her from eating the fruit, but not from possibly being tempted by touching the fruit. This is how Eve would have gotten this misrepresented information concerning God's command—through Adam. However, it is misleading due to the misrepresentation of God's command to Adam. Moses wrote of God's command to Adam, "Of every tree of the garden you may freely eat; but of the tree of knowledge of good and evil you shall not eat, for in the day that you eat of it you shall surely die."[21] The discussion of the tree's fruit by Satan is manipulative. The additional requirement "not to touch," stated by Eve, is recognition that the fruit is the fuel for Satan to use in his manipulation of Eve's deception and manipulation. The misrepresented information used for the purpose of causing doubt in God has become the catalyst for today's human downfall.

Today, this same manipulation is designed to devalue the scripture. This manipulation isolates us from the scripture's teaching and its impact upon us. The scriptures suggest that Satan set an example at the tree because Eve saw that the fruit was good for food.[22] It is at this point Eve was engaged and led toward the corruption of her innocence with Christ and Adam. The safety of any person who knows salvation stems from the foundation of the Bible, the example set by others, and the interactive relationship with Christ. There is a surety of the Bible having an impact upon people who are led toward salvation by lifting Christ up. However, the deception of Satan is manipulative, leading us away from God's commands, and his desire is for us—through this creation of doubt and the establishment of confusion—to violate them.

The second stage for the corruption of Eve's innocence is the depreciation of God's controlling authority. This corruption comes in direct opposition to God's authority by removing the support for his authority over Eve. Satan uses Eve's misinformation against her and depreciates God's authority in its wake. Satan says to Eve, "Has God indeed said?"[23] It is this questioning of God's authority that comes through Adam's additional requirement concerning not touching the fruit given to Eve. This manipulative questioning is what breeds the doubt concerning the fruit. The criteria for not eating the fruit involves the command given only to Adam,[24] not Eve. Thus, God specifically asks of Adam, "Have you eaten from the tree of which I commanded you that you should not eat?"[25] It was not until Adam ate of the fruit that both Eve's and Adam's eyes opened and the death by sin entered the world.

God's judgment came upon all humanity due to the violation of God's command and authority. Satan uses the misinformation Eve holds to his advantage by denying that the commandment poses any danger toward her or their relationship with God. Lucifer suggests that taking advantage of the opportunity to eat the fruit will be to her benefit. The replacement of God's authority ends in the direct violation of the command given by Adam to Eve. That is, an invalid curiosity concerning the fruit brings corruption through Satan's stating that Eve would be God's equal. This depreciation of God's authority through the misinformation by both Adam and Satan directly confronts God's status for Eve, which causes the erosion of Eve's support for Adam and creates doubt concerning the consequences of death decreed by God in its wake.

Satan needs to reeducate Eve for her corruption to take, and that leads to her getting involved. It is her participation in a corrupting practice that is required. This reeducation process produces an acceptance of deviant behavior, which leads to her own corruption. Of course, this process of corruption requires time to take place. Lucifer requires time for the reeducation of Eve and for the infusion and adoption of his manifesto. Some suggest Adam is near the tree during the discussion between Satan and Eve, listening to them. However, many commentaries suggest she is alone, away from her husband and a weaker vessel.[26] Of course, this brings new meaning to Paul's statement to the Corinthians: "Let each woman have her own husband."[27] Of course, Lucifer was not Eve's husband; however, he was the influence she listened to rather than her husband or Christ.

Eve is alone with Satan, listening to every word. In addition, Paul wrote regarding women, "If they want to learn something, let them ask their own husbands at home,"[28] and yet, Satan's deception takes place due to Eve's remaining inactive in her responsibility. This knavery will be the undoing of Adam and Eve. However, if Adam were there, the discussion of the fruit with Eve would not have occurred, or it would have been countered by Adam's knowledge of the commandment by God. Having already discussed the issue of the tree with Eve, he would have protected her from the influence of Satan at that moment. Paul writes to the Corinthians about the reeducation for Eve's corruption: "The serpent deceived Eve … corrupted from the simplicity that is in Christ."[29] Although Paul was using a metaphor regarding Eve and the craftiness of sin in our lives, dealt to us by Satan, this is the method Satan uses to manipulate Eve. The education of a sinful practice takes time to convey. Over time, the educational process requires an interactive exposure toward the active involvement for engageable and observable sinful behavior to take hold.

Lucifer's reeducation of Eve requires her to disregard God's authority. Eve throws aside the safety of established boundaries through the subversion of Satan's crafty words. Even today, words crafted to have trust and security within them but surrounded by deception using money, property, prestige, or even inclusion in manipulative ways brings about a disregarding of morality for the pleasure we receive. This develops an openness within Eve to sin without any restraint keeping her from doing it.

Lucifer, this evil teacher, develops sinful practices through the overt violation of established boundaries. And our acceptance of evil practices as normal is sin. The requirement for the alteration of sinful behavior of sin is repentance. The casting of doubt upon the righteous, holy, pure, or healthy, normal activities[30] requires the negation of established boundaries in exchange for the adoption of the evil concept of behavior and the application of the sinful practice. Setting an example of overt behavior in action makes the transition easier for others to follow. This engages the innocence, providing validation to them that it is perfectly fine to violate God's commands of ethical behavior. Paul rejects the issue of the educational injection of sin's acceptability and correctness. He wrote to the Colossians, "Beware, lest anyone cheat you through philosophy and empty deceit, according to the traditions of men, according to the basic principles of the world, and not according to Christ."[31] It is this corrupt educational process requiring acceptance of sinful practices that we see in Satan's corruption and deception of Eve.

Eve has to set aside her relationships for corruption to take place. Satan isolates Eve from the influences of Adam and Christ at the tree of knowledge. The conversation between Satan and Eve occurs at this tree all alone. Eve has already undergone the erosion of knowledge through Adam's misleading her. The ongoing relationship with God that has depreciated, being set aside, increases Satan's influence and authority as having supposed credibility with Eve. It is during this educational phase that Satan becomes an overt behavioral teacher. This changes Eve's focus on the fruit; the scripture saying that she "saw that the tree was good for food … pleasant to the eyes, and … desirable to make one wise"[32] shows us so. Without Satan's example in action, and without Christ or Adam there, she could not have seen that the fruit was good, pleasant, and desirable.

This process of reeducation had to take a large amount of time while she was isolated. After Eve's reeducation is accomplished through the observation of Satan's actions and she accepts the evidence that eating the fruit of the tree of knowledge is not a problem, action on her part is still a required addition for corruption to take place. This evidence is based on the false premise that she can be like God and—when combined with both true and false arguments of the fruit's being good to eat, beautiful, delicious for wisdom, and a way to avoid death—is the deception that corrupts Eve. Eve is not an isolated case. Her reeducated condition of desire and removal from the safety of her healthy relationships, leading toward corruption, are in everyday life today.

Cults use reeducation to promote deceptive manipulative exchanges. They present an appealing opening that leads to the isolation of an individual. The focus is on those who feel separated from the influence of Christian believers or the Bible, isolated from a course toward God. This process draws the lonely into their folds through this reeducation. Then the foundation of faith, the Bible, is removed, and the influence of faith by those honoring it is accomplished. It is through this isolation and ignorant knavery that the removal of this foundation of authority occurs. Safety in reeducation requires that the neonate's corruption be an ever-deepening mandatory process over time. Before the acceptance and engagement involving a sinful practice, it requires a promotion of these sinful practices to be appropriate and in a form of normalized and acceptable behavior.

Finally, the innocent victim must act upon this reeducated

behavior. James had it right: "When desire has conceived, it gives birth to sin; and sin, when it is full-grown, brings forth death."[33] Eve must accept the false premise Lucifer has presented and his overt argument that she will not die and will be like God. Satan challenges the commandment from Adam and tempts Eve by drawing her "away by [her] own desires and enticed"[34] with the future possibility of being God's equal. She willfully forgets Adam's commandment due to Satan's argument that disputes the fruit and God's credibility. Eve's place is the support for Adam, as his helpmate, which includes helping him stay away from the fruit. This purpose of Eve is then tarnished and corrupted. She reaches out, takes the fruit, and eats it.[35] Eve becomes corrupted in her support for Adam by acting upon Satan's deception and manipulated misinformation about eating the fruit. This corrupts Adam's understanding of God's command. Eve becomes the first easy prey who adopts Satan's mission.

Eve took the mantle of Satan's manifesto. This is a harsh thing to suggest about the mother of all humankind. People consider Eve to be innocent of the charges of sin. Even in the face of Satan's corruption of her from being the support for Adam, we could and can consider her free of evil with regard to eating the fruit. However, Satan's corruption comes from the false premise, "You shall not surely die, for God knows that in the day you eat of it, then your eyes will be opened, and you shall be as God, knowing good and evil."[36] This is Satan's goal of being God's equal passed to Eve through eating the fruit.

Eve forgets her place as Adam's support. God never condemns her for eating of the fruit of the tree of good and evil.[37] He never charges her with condemnation or judgment for the consumption of the fruit. In fact, God says to the woman, "What is this you have done?"[38] No command was given to Eve about not eating the fruit, but God's command confronted Adam's behavior. This is not the issue of common sinful behavior, found in the commandments,[39] which is after the fact of sin's infusion into the lives of Adam and Eve. However, written in Genesis 3:6, Eve ate the fruit after being exposed to Satan's activities at the tree. Although Adam has no immunity in eating the fruit, it is as if this Jehovah Elohiym had granted Eve the ability to eat of the fruit with impunity.

This points out the issue that a command given by God to one person may not be the same as that given to another. Each is one person God sends to one place for a purpose in life with the gifts for doing a particular ministry, while another's purpose is to go there with these gifts for another ministry. If they do not attend to what they are sent to do, then sin enters and the flaw is not following what God has commanded of them to do. This does not distract us from the ongoing requirements of God's standards of conduct for all people, nor does it lack the power of the law to condemn sin in our lives for the things we do in the flesh. In this case, the commandment not to eat was given to Adam, not to Eve. Eve was built for the support of Adam; she was a helpmate for Adam's good pleasure and help. It was Lucifer who corrupted the standards and purposes given to Eve at the tree for the union and harmony with Adam.

Satan corrupts good habits of the innocent. Satan attacked Adam's weakest point—his support, who was Eve, his helpmate. It was this false premise of being God's equal, which is the foundation of his manifesto.[40] This came while this created being called Satan—or in this case, the serpent, one of God's archangels—was in a position of authority in the heavens. This coupled with Satan's overt persuasion at the tree corrupted Eve. When Eve concluded the fruit was good for the satisfaction of the lust of her eyes and flesh and for the pride in life,[41] she ate it. This removal of Adam's support through Eve's deception and subsequent corruption created an overt deception for Adam, believing what was being said to her was true. Thus, the false premise presented to Eve became the foundation of Adam's doubt. She ate of the fruit believing Satan's credentials as he presented them. She doubted God's credibility and Adam's misrepresentation of knowledge concerning her responsibility and the fruit. Through Satan's deceptive manipulation, this knave mother of humanity believed Satan's false premise for being like God and ate the fruit of the tree of knowledge.

Eve shared the fruit with Adam. This is a normal action between children, having an experience and wanting to share it with friends. Eve, having been deceived and corrupted, made a conclusion about the fruit and passed the fruit to Adam. She caused Adam to doubt God's command through her example, and he took the fruit and ate of it. Adam disbelieved God concerning the coming of death when he ate the fruit. Yet it was not until he assumed that Eve was the overt example of what was to happen after eating of the fruit that he overruled God's command by doubting it. It was at this point that Adam's command from God was in doubt because he had seen Eve eat the fruit and not die. This doubt concerning God's command and Eve's observable action through Lucifer's manipulation, which appeared to give her permission to eat the fruit, were the deceptive results for Adam. It is unknown whether Adam came on the scene to see Eve still holding the eaten fruit in her hand, with fruit in her mouth, or with her showing him the result of her action. But the point is that the support intended to help Adam maintain the commandment of God was tainted, deceived, and corrupted.

Adam believed Eve over God's command upon him. Paul understood the deception of corruption in our lives today. He wrote about Eve and wrote concerning us, "I fear lest by any means, as the serpent beguiled Eve in his craftiness, so your thoughts should be corrupted from the simplicity due to Christ."[42] The companion for every Christian is the word of God, the Bible, which never changes in the study from one person to the next. There can be no private interpretation of scripture, and scripture's confirmation comes through the Holy Spirit's[43] revelation to us. When we are deceived, like Adam in believing Eve, we believe the lie concerning the scripture. Furthermore, Paul wrote to Timothy concerning the issue: "All scripture is God-breathed, and is profitable for doctrine, for reproof, for correction, for instruction in righteousness, that the man of God may be perfected, thoroughly furnished to every good work."[44] Eve created doubt for Adam, and in the shock of this doubt, Adam ate the fruit.

Satan deceives us by removing our foundation of scripture. He then deceives and corrupts us[45] through the process of removing from us the authority of the word of God. It is upon this false foundation that the minions of Satan weave a good replacement. This replacement has both elements of the truth and the fabrication of lies, just like the serpent of old, which is accepted as valid and true. Lucifer is an evil companion corrupting good habits. This serpent of old, Satan, replaces God's authority with a false premise, creating doubt for the foundation of scripture to support his argument of being God's equal. He does this by exchanging the facts, exchanging the truth with both false and true arguments, and then using this deception and manipulation to propagate his manifesto. This manipulation born for our corruption takes the place of God. We become as his equal, and we depreciate God's status in our lives. Therefore, the removal of the basic study, reading, and evaluation of the scripture is the removal of the food we need in life that is replaced with being God's equal in life.

CHAPTER 2

EZEKIEL 37:15-28—AN UNFULFILLED PROPHETIC MESSAGE

> **And you, son of man, take a stick and write on it, For Judah and his companions, the sons of Israel. And take another stick and write on it, For Joseph, the stick of Ephraim, and all the house of Israel, his companions. (Ezekiel 37:16 NKJV)**

Prophecy has been an area of misrepresentation over the years. Some believe that having a success rate of less than 100 percent in determining future events is acceptable. However, in God's universe, false prophets are those who predict future events that do not happen. In God's course of events, what is spoken of in prophecy does not come back void. However, there is accomplishment in a situation of which God has spoken before it happens. The above quote from Ezekiel 37:15–28 is an unfulfilled prophetic message—one that is yet to occur that cannot be anything but what it is stated to be. It is an explicit prophecy when God defines what the answer is to be.

A prophecy is an utterance from God. Prophecy is an endowed discourse of divine inspiration for the declaration of God's purposes. The terms used for this type of declaration in scripture suggest that prophecy is a form of prediction. Prophecy is a superior, inspired heralding of things. It is a lifted foretelling that exposes events, situations, results, blessings, or judgments upon a person, a place, or a people. It is a manifesting and illumination of information to show what is to be or what shines upon the hearer. It can be meant to reprove a person, place, or community or to admonish the wicked. The prophetic message can comfort the afflicted or reveal things that are hidden. This forewarning can be the foretelling of future events, the prediction of events pending, or the details of works to be done by God. Isaiah quoted Jehovah, writing, "So shall My Word be, which goes out of My mouth; it shall not return to Me void, but it shall accomplish what I please, and it shall certainly do what I sent it to do."[46] The burden of any prophetic utterance is for it to be what God has called it to be and nothing more.

It is this bold ability to declare the truth of God's handiwork that makes it unique. It calls people to be righteous and adjust to a holy life, regardless of the consequences. Prophecy is for rooting out and pulling down the structures of sin for their removal. It can destroy and throw down sin's authority, or it can dissolve its influence.[47] It can build up or plant the restoration of a new life. It has the integrity for living life according to God's standards,[48] based upon God's judgment and accounting of each of us. Isaiah wrote, "I have declared the former things from the beginning; they went forth from My mouth, and I caused them to hear it. Suddenly, I did them, and they came to pass."[49] The issue for humankind with prophecy is the foundation of God's capability of doing exactly what he says he will do.

Prophecy will accomplish exactly what God has sent it to do. This type of prophetic message can be no different from the message given. It has specific details, which require it to be what it is and nothing more. It cannot be any alternative message, lesson, or application gleaned from it before its completion. Humankind cannot remember the past and will not be here into the hereafter to see the future come into existence.[50] Prophecy reveals the past and declares the end of the prophetic message, which is upon all people and things to come.[51] God speaks, saying, "Behold, the former things have come to pass, and new things I declare; before they happen, I cause you to hear."[52] God has planned a thing, done a thing, called forth the generation for the thing, and qualified it from the beginning with effectiveness in its accomplishment.

The prophetic message concerning the hope of eternal life comes through Jesus Christ. This is because of a God who promised eternal life before eternal times and cannot lie.[53] Satan is a created being, and his works are nothing more than lying corruption. Lucifer's pride in thinking he can become God's equal has made him a being of abominable words and actions. He has become nothing, thinking he is everything, and the future includes casting him into the pit for retention in fulfilling the sentence. He attempts to corrupt the foundations of God for humankind. However, this great God, the everlasting God who is our savior, our adoptive parent, tries to communicate with us about the issues in our lives. This Jehovah Elohiym, Jesus Christ, has allowed others to write down prophetic messages through the work of forty authors in sixty-six books that are combined into one work. He says to us, "Come now, and let us reason together.... Though your sins are like scarlet, they shall be as white as snow; though they are red like crimson, they shall be as wool."[54] It is this reasoning together that makes the aftermath that the *Christian Study Bible* translates as, "Come, now, let us settle the question," the conclusion fixed together between two people. God never spoke a prophetic message in secrecy.[55] He does speak of eternal life through Christ, but not in secret.

The possession of salvation comes before our existence. It is this possession of our salvation through Jesus Christ, established and presented before the foundation of the earth, that is intended for us as a gift. He gave to us this inheritance of faith before the eternal times began, making it premeditated. This was Christ's purpose for us and the grace granted to us.[56] It is this great God, Jesus Christ of Nazareth, who defines himself as the first and the last. This great God of salvation is Christ, this Jehovah Elohiym,[57] who provides our salvation through his blood shed on the cross as the lamb of God. This Jesus, who was "before all things and by him all things exist,"[58] is the God of prophecy. Jehovah defines the beginning from the end and does not do it in secret; he is priest, king, and the counsel of peace.[59] God's purpose shall stand, and it will do his good pleasure.[60] Jesus's counsel stands forever[61] and is wonderful in wisdom[62] and excellent in guidance. There is no other God beside Jesus, who saves people through the remission of their sins[63] and is complete in the work. We can come face to face with the God of creation, who is this Jesus, the Jehovah Elohiym. This Jesus Christ of Nazareth makes our sins white as snow as we reason with him and repent. Jesus Christ is the God of our salvation, bringing us salvation from before the foundations of the earth.

Scripture is a luminary into God's ways. The psalmist wrote, "Your Word is a lamp to my feet, and a light to my path."[64] Satan attempts to corrupt us through the shadow of doubt and our ignorance. However, Paul wrote to Timothy, "All scripture is God-breathed, and is profitable for doctrine, for reproof, for correction, for instruction in righteousness, that the man of God may be perfected, thoroughly furnished to every good work."[65] Of course, Satan wants to add, change, distract, and replace God's word for something corrupted. To achieve his purposes of being God's equal or taking God's place in our lives, corruption needs to take place. Satan's minions attempt to take away the Bible's impact, which is the foundation of our interaction with God, Christ, and the Holy Spirit. Jehovah speaks concerning his word, saying, "I will watch over my Word to perform it."[66] The serpent of old tries to degrade this building block of faith in Christ—faith that comes through the stability of the scriptures as surety of life. The removal of scripture then corrupts our faith with doubt because "faith is of hearing, and hearing by the Word of God."[67] The removal of this stability of our moral definition, damaging our relationship with Christ, comes through the infusion of the sin of doubt, thus affecting our relationships with those around us. This is Satan's manifesto process, removing the support for our salvation stemming from scripture. The scripture displays the salvation of God through Christ, which is his process of delivery to those of us in the future, while its removal leads toward corruption.

There are prophetic messages concerning Christ, and they put Christ's lordship over the ownership of all his creation. However, Satan's manifesto attempts to remove the prophetic foundation of scripture, which provides the written accounting of it. The corruption of the scripture makes the speaking of Christ's prophetic messages unstable, misrepresented, and despised. This corruption of the scripture becomes an unsuitable format for the prophetic message, allowing the rewriting of the accounts. What will come into the minds of humankind concerning the fantasy and acceptable fallacies of doubting the scripture is the corruption of something being God's equal or replacement. The dissuasion from scripture causes the isolation of people from coming to Christ and accepting the salvation provided through faith.

The discrediting of Christ has discouraged the masses from having faith in him. The loss of the scripture's value impacts our lives, leaving them a thwarted and twisted corruption of the soul. Even though the constituent validity, the mass rule, concerning the scripture may become tainted, corrupt, infused with sin, and filled with acceptable sin, the scripture remains stable and true. This means a distortion, misrepresentation, or deception of our lives comes in the wake of our doubt in it. The replacements of scripture always take us away from the validity that is due Christ in our living worship. For example, there is a blessing for the person who reads John's book of Revelation concerning Jesus Christ and keeps the things written in it.[68] In addition, there is a warning as well. This warning comes for anyone adding to or taking away from the prophecy contained in the Revelation[69] of Christ. Furthermore, the blessing given for keeping "the words of the prophesy of the Book"[70] is not sealed up but is for everyone reading it. The prophetic message is given because the "time is at hand."[71] It is to understand the importance of Christ's surety in this world and the prophecies concerning him. So when we come to the foundation of scripture found in Revelation, written by John, we face the prophetic message of Christ's eminent future for both believers and unbelievers.

The prophet's character is the witnessing of Jesus. The results of the work of faith stem from the power of scriptures revealing the love story of salvation through Christ. This faith becomes the characteristic of the prophet's power and character. We will define *prophecy* as written in Revelation 19:10: the "testimony of Jesus is the spirit of prophecy."[72] There is a point when God and prophecy require us to have faith in Christ. This prophecy and faith become our focus and our attention as believers in Christ, uniting us all. Even Moses wrote, "Oh, that all the Lord's people were prophets and that the Lord would put His Spirit upon them!"[73] Prophecy is the sensible exaltation of praise brought with the breath of speech and presentation. It is this prophetic nature of this up-and-coming prophecy that concerns the day of redemption, which qualifies our faith in Christ for salvation as valid.

A prophet's courage stems from the faith in God's character. The faith of the prophet has the characteristic of lacking fear or despair. This leaves the prophet with animation in life, stemming from a lively faith in God's abilities. One might say the prophet has a slight dramatic flair. The exuberance of the prophet comes from the quality filling of God's spirit. The prophet is both called and filled. The prophet has a character tempered with the congruence of righteous conduct and the power from God, himself.

The vigor of the prophet is intense. He or she has a force of active strength and the energy of body and mind. The administration of power gives him energy in life from the "shikeanah" glory of God's presence. This exemplification of the glory of God is the same glory that surrounded Mount Sinai, that is present during the time of the temple sacrifice, or that fills the believer from Christ. The prophet's disposition of character has a natural attitude toward things in an arranged tendency according to God's standards and requirements. The character of this consistency of God in the life of a prophet fills him with the courage to do the required dissemination from God, despite whatever consequences might occur.

Faith comes from hearing the word of prophecy. Faith is God's accomplishment as our author and finisher of our faith; binding the foundation of the believer's faith to the word of scripture is its accomplishment. The hearing of the word brings with it stabilization in our lives and desire to act accordingly. Due to the scripture's unchanged nature, we receive the perfect law of God, which converts our soul.[74] The testimony of the scripture makes us wise because the scripture is like Jehovah himself[75] and unchanging. The statues or precepts, these commandments of direction for the rule of action and conduct of our lives, coming from Jehovah are right,[76] bringing us peace in life. This causes our behavior to become straight and upright, making our heart rejoice and making life lighter and easier to bear.[77] The commandments given us help to enjoin our constitution with clarity and with an examination of the quality of our purity toward him. They give us light, and this light produces understanding and enlightenment. This understanding and enlightenment show us how to live our lives in righteousness.[78] Faith is the process of hearing the word of God that leads us to Christ, converting our souls, changing the character of our lives, and allowing us to live in peace with God in the purity of a congruent integrity.

This produces respect for God through Christ. It is the foundation upon which a sound innocence becomes placed within us and is an unadulterated conscience that endures forever. This respect we glean from Christ awakens in us because of the scripture's cleaning impact upon our hearts. The validity of the scripture improves our relationship with God, our Father in heaven, and Christ.[79] This privileged verdict of God's justice clearly stabilizes our lives to build and support moral uprightness according to his judgment.[80] The psalmist has it right concerning the scripture and our relationship with Christ, writing, "Let the words of my mouth, and the meditation of my heart be pleasing in Your sight, O Jehovah, my Rock, and my Redeemer."[81] My repentance, when based upon scripture, aligns my life with God's truth and righteousness. The foundation of scripture produces one mind that animates the church into acting as one body, in one faith, with one God, and with the one Lord, who is Jesus Christ of Nazareth. Repentance aligns us with God's standards with Christ as the truth of prophecy, being holy and righteous, building our faith and judging our lives.

Application of Fulfilled Prophesy

> **Worship God, for the testimony of Jesus is the spirit of prophecy.**[82]

The application of fulfilled prophesy is for building our personal lives. This is the nature of prophecy that already has occurred, and its application is for everyday life. After the fulfillment of an explicit prophesy, the application of the dynamics of behavior involved in the prophetic message applied to our daily living is both rewarding and educational.

Some explicit prophecies are historical in nature. This type of prophetic message cannot be anything other than what it was in life. In addition, fulfilled prophetic messages provide for us an exhibition of God's character, actions, and expectations of us as a historic experience. Prophecy is a procurement of action upon a living soul, group of people, or place. After the completion of judgment or blessing enacted through prophecy, the dynamics of the behavior eliciting either judgment or blessing applied to our own lives are life changing.

Our first example is the churches of Revelation. When John wrote the book of Revelation, each church had its own prophetic message. These churches had issues ofbehavior, weaknesses, strengths, commendations, judgments upon them, and a prophetic message concerning them. However, the churches no longer exist. They succumbed to later experiences, which led to their disappearance from the world scene, and only their remains are left. However, as we read, study, and apply the prophetic message contained in the dynamics of each church, we glean a rich theme for today's behavioral requirements and judgment upon our own personal lives, the church's activities, the impact within the community, the state's governance, the country's status, and even the world at large. Thus, fulfilled prophesy brings to us a richness of God's power of forethought, power of action, and the quality of application into our daily lives, which develops an ongoing intimate relationship with Christ concerning our behavior.

The second type of prophetic message concerns the conditional consequences of behavior. This type of prophetic message concerns the nature of the behavior and then pronounces a consequence. In Exodus 15:26, Moses wrote of this type of prophetic example, "If you will diligently head the voice the Lord your God, and do what is right in His sight, give ear to his commandments, and keep all his statutes, I will put none of the diseases on you, which I have brought upon the Egyptians; for I am the Lord, who heals you."[83] In addition, Deuteronomy 28 details daily living conditions, requiring our adherence to the call to righteousness and calling it a blessing. The disqualification of our behavior requires that we receive consequences at the time, calling it judgment or cursing. These types of behavior-qualified prophetic messages of blessing or cursing concern the keeping of God's standards of living.

One more example is God's statement of dedication, one of which was given to the Israelites and which we can apply to ourselves when we follow the directions. The prophets of Ezekiel, Isaiah, and Hosea had ministries that addressed sin and judgment. In addition, another example of prophetic conditioned response is in Romans 10:9–10, where Paul wrote, "If you confess the Lord Jesus, and believe in your heart that God has raised him from the dead, you shall be saved. For with the heart, one believes unto righteousness, and with the mouth one confesses unto salvation." Revelation 20:15 falls into this category as well: "If anyone was not found having been written in the Book of Life, he was cast into the Lake of Fire." These conditional prophesies are demanding ones that end in either tormented death for eternity or a peaceful life with Christ and the Father of heaven. The judgments were and are explicit. Their aftermath is the lesson for behavioral correctness and judgment upon sinful interactions. Their consequences occur if we do not follow the standards of purity and holiness with God or if we meet God's requirements for behavior. Those who met the requirements of either blessing or cursing show this form of dedicated prophetic message.

Explicitness of Unfulfilled Prophesy

> **So, we have the prophetic word confirmed, which you do well to heed as a light that shines in a dark place, until the day dawns and the morning star rises in the hearts; knowing this first, that no prophecy of scripture is of any private interpretation, for prophesy never came by the will of man, but holy men of God spoke as they were moved by the Holy Spirit.[84]**

The opposite is true for explicit unfulfilled prophecy. Satan attempts to stop this type of prophetic message by changing its formula. This type of spoken prophecy suggests something different in the wake of the deception causing its change. Thus, attempting to thwart God's prophetic message creates a depreciation of God's character and his consistency in our lives.

Christ then becomes flawed in our eyes. At times, we can apply to our lives the required repentance or the changes in our behavior stemming from the gleaned knowledge of a passage of prophecy. It is when we do so that we have an interactive impact with God. However, we glean from this type of prophetic message hope or the need for repentance. The knowledge of the condemnation of judgment coming from unaltered sin requires repentance. There can be either judgment or blessing upon our own behavioral involvement with sin, or there is an application of the prophetic message upon our lives with its focus in righteousness. It is here that many people think judgement is nonexistent. It is as if some people could live without God's judgment while sin runs rampant. However, you can never take a prophetic message out of the context of its future event. Any attempt at making a private interpretation of this type of future prophetic message turns it into something other than its intended purpose. Prophetic messages cannot be anything other than what they are.

The prophetic message of Ezekiel 37:15–28 is one of these unfulfilled prophecies. For example, the book of Ezekiel is not the only place where this prophecy is written. The many different variants to Ezekiel's unfulfilled prophecy validate the prophetic message. This is still for fulfillment in future time as defined through scripture. This means Ezekiel's prophecy, written as is, is explicit. Ezekiel's prophecy follows the normal Jewish teaching style. This teaching style involves an initialization of the topic, which requires waiting for a response to the statement.[85] We see this type of teaching in Genesis 1:1–2 as well. This is laying the foundation of a topic that God is forcing us to examine. So when people ask what this prophecy means, the explanation comes in a basic, simplified format for them to understand.[86] Again, we see this same process of teaching in Genesis 1:3–31, as God develops the living world containing the creation of humankind, stemming from God's creating the heavens and the earth. Finally, the final phase of this teaching style defines this prophetic message in fullness. The prophetic message comes during the last statement concerning the kingdom of God and the throne of David.[87] Furthermore, in Genesis 2, we see the final topic of creation's focus as the part of creation where God creates Adam and Eve in the unity of marriage and in the purity of a face-to-face relationship with Christ. In this aftermath of these two examples of teaching, this prophecy cannot be anything but what God says it will be in the future.

The example of Ezekiel's prophecy is the establishment of David's throne forever. Isaiah wrote about a child born with the government on his shoulder; this is Christ.[88] David's throne had been established with judgment, justice, and peace, and this is the focus of this prophecy. Worship in this city is forever and will come from every part of the world to praise Jehovah.[89] Jesus is the branch grown up to David. Our righteousness because of him will cause us to make sacrifices forever with the priest and Levites[90] in the city called Jehovah. David will be set up as shepherd and ruler over them, and Jehovah will be their God.[91] It will be at the end of days, with Jehovah as their God and David as their king.[92] This covenant with David will never break and will continue, while the number of children will be immeasurable.[93] This covenant with David is an established seed forever, building his throne in all generations.[94] Jehovah will defend his people as he destroys the nations coming against Jerusalem. He will pour out on the house of David the spirit of grace and prayer.[95] The extent of Ezekiel's prophecy and all the supporting scripture provides evidence that this explicit prophecy can be only what it says it is for us and will be as a future event.

CHAPTER 3

THE INFUSION OF SIN ON NATURE

He who practices sin is of the Devil, for the Devil sins from the beginning. For this purpose, the Son of God was revealed, that he might undo the works of the Devil.[96]

Ever since Adam and Eve, with their face-to-face walk with Christ in the garden, sin has been encoded into our nature because of their fall. This encoding of infused sin into our behavior progressively occurs as we develop and change over time and causes corruption of our God consciences, attempting to force it into nonexistence. The reeducation of our souls from our God consciences toward godlessness is the consequence visited upon humanity. The filter of having godly parents limits the extent of this failure toward a God conscience. In addition, having impressionable mentors during our lives leaves us in better places, understanding, and awareness of this God conscience. However, our sin nature has limits within us in validating this God conscience.

A God conscience counteracts our sin nature. The impregnation upon our natures with sin demands a means for remission of our sin. Many times, this leads to seeking justification of our sin and behavior, which is self-justification. The sin and behavior against God's standards attempt the deflection of the seriousness of our condition, seeking through our own means and capability in reducing its impact. Although Christ has provided a means of atonement for the remission of our sins, the infusion of sin raises contempt, an ire of refusal, and rebelliousness of nonacceptance for this atonement. Sin has the characteristic of changing our nature and lives, which infused into our souls long ago with the initial corruption and lead to destruction.

Judgment upon sin was not exclusive to human existence. God did not spare the sinning angels, who were filled with their pride and left their first home. These angels followed Satan, believing his manifesto of being God's equal and replacement. These angels, reserved for judgment in the great day,[97] are in chains of darkness forever.[98] They have already been judged with a pending sentence awaiting to be carried out in future events and are corrupting future companions.

Examples of judgment upon sin have been ongoing. In the days of Noah, God did not spare the world, but only this preacher of righteousness and his family survived. When the flood destroyed the world of its continuous evil and its people, judgment came upon the thoughts and the hearts of humankind for the completion to sin's[99] judgment. However, judgment does not fix the condition of human hearts. Christ qualifies our present time as being the same as the days of Noah.[100,101,102] God's long-suffering at the time of Noah prepared only eight people for salvation from the flood.

Yes, we had the sentence of death in ourselves, that we should not trust in ourselves, but in God, who raises from the dead, who delivers us from so great a death, and does delivers us; in whom we trust that he will still deliver us.[103]

God reserves the sin nature for the day of judgment's punishment. Furthermore, in judging humankind's sinful actions, God turned his attention to the cries against Sodom and Gomorrah.[104] The cry was so great and so very grievous regarding their ungodly living that it demanded destruction. God delivered Lot, like Noah, from the lustful behavior of the lawlessness along with his compromising behavior through association with their sinful practices. God judged Sodom and Gomorrah without mercy, like the flood, for the torment of their unlawful deeds upon the righteous. Christ knows how to deliver us from our temptations and, thus, from the day of judgment, providing a means of escape for us all.[105] Therefore, we do not have to end in judgment for our sin and can escape to a life of redemption.

Balaam is our final example here of the wages of unrighteousness. He sought to gain money for profit by cursing the Israelites, and instead, he told Amalek how sin would entice and cause God to curse his own people. The qualifying of unrighteousness requires the definition of an indulgence through an inappropriate pleasure. This is a revealing of a simple spot or blemishes upon our character and has deceit at its core. The judgment upon our behavior is the price of unrighteousness.

Sin has the same ending every time. No matter the degree of sin, the wages of sin is the same, ending in death. "There is none righteous, no not one; there is none that understands, there is none that seeks after God."[106] The nature of sin and its characteristics have only this one theme in common. No matter the level of the sin or its vileness, it consummates in one statement: "All unrighteousness is sin."[107] We levitate our sinful actions to the level of obscurity, while our chosen sinful actions become acceptable. However, "Whoever commits sin, also commits lawlessness, and sin is lawlessness."[108] The deceitfulness of sin, however small and humanly insignificant it might be, hardens the heart against God and his word.[109] Jesus spoke of the nature of sin, saying, "Whoever practices sin is the slave of sin,"[110] making the practice of sin, however small, slavery. Sin changes the glory of righteousness into shame, setting the heart toward iniquity.[111] We qualify ourselves in our own eyes, defining ourselves by our own terms of behavior. It is the nature and obsession of sinful humans to justify ourselves in the sin, which leads to the same ending of death.

We never consider ourselves sinful. Sin replaces Christ as God. Sin discredits righteous living, or Christ, by lying that the scripture is inadequate and corrupted. This leads people to all kinds of lust for power and authority behind the corruption.[112] This sells us under the curse of our sin[113]; we succumb to "the sting of death, for the strength of sin is the Law."[114] God knows his own mind about redemption for us: "I will purge out from among you the rebels and those who sin against me. I will bring them out from the land where they reside, and they shall not enter the land of Israel. You shall know that I am Jehovah."[115] Although God is talking about Israel, we can see this same interactive condition with those of us who are not Israelites. God does not accept sinful practices as honorable, righteous, or holy. He separates himself from the sin and from those who reject him. Thus, Paul makes the point, "Let not anyone deceive you by any means. For that day shall not come unless there first comes a falling away."[116] People cannot reject the Bible or Christ unless they have already begun falling away through their sin nature. Sin always involves falling away from God when there is no repentance.

We are prejudiced in our sin. The pride of prejudice is the fruition of sin, suggesting that we are better than another human being. Our status as believers or nonbelievers makes us feel somehow superior to the next sinner in life. This can happen through refuting scripture, discrediting morality, decreasing God's authority and status, justifying ourselves, attempting to be God's equal, and qualifying our standards by our own designs. In addition, it comes as the rejection of Christ to forgive sin. James knew this when he wrote, "Each one is tempted when he is drawn away by his own desire and enticed. Then, when desire has conceived, it gives birth to sin, and sin, when it is full-grown, brings forth death."[117] Therefore, relief comes from the only mediator, Jesus Christ, who is God and capable of forgiving sin. The scripture promises, "The scripture has confined all under sin, that the promise by faith in Jesus Christ might be given to those, who believe."[118] This is the nature of the infusion of sin into our character by Satan's manifesto in Genesis and its only relief through Christ. Our sin, however insignificant, is lawlessness and rebellion against God, requiring Christ to atone for the remission of our sin.

Nature of Sin

> **Homosexuality is NOT a sin. Atheism is NOT a sin. Belonging to the wrong religion is NOT a sin. You know why? Because sin is an imaginary disease invented to sell you an imaginary cure. — SomeKindaLeftist_2017d**

The nature of sin has characteristics we can observe. The sin's nature follows Satan's manifesto in denying Christ and his authority. It calls impurity and sin acceptable behavior. This puffed-up condition of godhood creates a position of superiority and self-justification. We desire to sail away into a living paradise defined by our own desires and lust. This sinful character raises one up to disunion within the relationship between Christ and humankind. The formula disqualifying God's standards promotes our own standards as better and accepted, as normal, but not found in scripture. These destructive heresies have a delusion of personal grandeur. Lifting ourselves up into righteousness through our own design is delusion. The acts from our sin nature run to ruin and loss, which destroy our lives.

When we sin, we perish. We lose the best part of living—that is, our own souls—in the process. Destructive heresies come into our lives with secrecy and isolation. The things done in secrecy come from false teachers or false prophets attempting to lead people away from the foundation of their faith or truth about their faith. This causes a deportation from faith with a rejection of scripture. Thus, the separation from scripture allows us to give "heed to deceiving spirits and doctrines of demons, speaking lies in hypocrisy, having their own conscience seared with a hot iron."[119] Although many do not go into the depths that the vileness of sin can produce, the attempt to measure the depths of sin is critiqued, saying one behavior is not as bad as another. This comes not from measuring ourselves against the standards of God found in scripture but from redefining the standards in our own eyes, disqualifying the scripture. Every measurement of sin that man redefines is an attempt to lessen the degree of the consequence God has imposed it. The shame stemming from the behavior and the guilt associated with violating God's standards is incredibly painful. Therefore, there is an evil speaking of the truth, calling it vile, calling it irresponsible, calling it futile, and not made for today's chosen behaviors of acceptable sin.

The consideration of the scripture becomes inadequate. This deception is, in its simplest form, a distortion corrupting the truth. A covetousness for God's standing exists in the world. Some attempt to gain status by using well-formulated words and arguments to prove this. These arguments dispel the concept of God's judgment upon the nature of our sin. This then disqualifies the need for a place of punishment or even atonement for sin. This refutes the scripture, and we accept it. This defense of refuting Christ or refuting the scripture concerning our nature of sin results in the peril of an illusion of advancement in our own eyes.

The pending judgment upon sin does not sleep. Without Christ, the consequences of judgment accumulate until the day judgment comes to us face to face and we are face to face with Christ. Then, this judgment requires full payment based upon God's terms and standards. As with many sins, we experience an immediate consequence in the physical sense, but with God, there comes a day of reckoning. "Jehovah is known. He has executed judgment; the wicked is snared in the work of his own hands."[120] In addition, "Let destruction come upon him, he will not know; and let his net, which he has concealed catch him, let him fall in it, into destruction."[121] When faced with our own destruction due to our sin, our sin nature, or our sinful actions, sin catches us in our own desires and lust; and with them comes the pending of our own destruction. However, "when the wicked springs as the grass, and when all the workers of iniquity blossom, it is they shall be destroyed forever."[122] Our condemnation comes as a consequence of our own actions of behavior.[123] We then impatiently await judgment's penalty.

In addition, the sin nature is after the flesh. The flesh has a lust from the corruption contaminating our relationship with God and depreciating our morals. Our ability to make amends for this sin founded upon the limitations of our relationship with Christ demands intercession. Many times, the sin nature characterized by a despising of government or authority over us is rebellion at its core. Of course, this authority over us comes in the form of God's status with us. Thus, self-willed, audacious people speak evil of dignity and dignitaries upholding morality. Such were the people who were against Christ. The sin nature causes people to speak evil of things they do not understand and then perish in their own corruption. They become brutish, unreasoning animals born into the captivity of sin and corruption. This is the nature of sinful flesh and unbelief.

So many times, corruption comes from the simplistic forms of sin. This allows a persistent acceptance of sin as appropriately normal. Sin has eyes full of adultery, which is idolatry. Although we may not have an active attraction for people other than our mates, the idolatry is the nature of a sinful practice[124, 125] and we accept it as perfectly normal. Sin is part of the nature of idolatry, of attempting to make us God's equal or replacement, of or just plain replacing him with something from the creation. This is the corruption coming from the simplicity of sin's lack of the scripture and Christ in one's life.

It is the covetousness of one's character that makes sin's nature so prevalent. This type of corruption leads people astray, like Eve in the beginning with Satan. The spirit of God is not in them. Thus, driven by the storms of feelings and shame, the reservation of blackness and darkness is forever. The character of sin comes with great swelling words of vanity, lust of the flesh, and unbridled addictions. Not having fully known the way of righteousness, vanity delivers them to the mire of the vomit of their sin nature. This enslavement blinds them to the entanglement of the things within sin's deception. The lust promises liberty only to enslave them in the corruption.

The Core of Deception

> **But let your word be, yes, yes; no, no. For whatever is more than these comes from evil.[126]**

The confrontation of deception in the world is an ongoing issue of life. Circular reasoning is one of the core deceptions we place on ourselves. One can examine the world of cults and see that this deception comes without a foundation of scripture. At the core of deception are the depths of an acceptable sin that includes removing scripture's validity. The denial of Christ's fulfillment of atonement for sin is the nature of the rebellion of deception. At the depths of depravity in this world, we find deception mixed in. The issues of deception become the forefront lines between good and evil. Deception is a form of dishonesty that is undisclosed and many times hidden from view, accepted as valid or rational. It assumes the appearance of something that is not and hides itself in similar words with different meanings and criteria. The law of deception defines the premise of an argument as being based on a lie and having its foundation in critical thinking born in dishonesty. The core of deception is just this, a mixture of the truth with lies passed off as accurate and valid while based on a false claim.

Deceit is nothing new in our world. The first deception, one might say, was Jacob, a son of Isaac. Jacob, considered a heel catcher[127] when he was born,[128] was the first notated deceiver. Jacob wanted to have Esau's birthright and, with his mother's counsel, stole Esau's blessing. Although Jacob took Esau's inheritance through manipulative domination using a source of food, he also deceived Isaac, his father, and took Esau's blessing from him. The word for *deceit* for this story[129] is *mirmah*,[130] which means to deceive or defraud. The trickery and pretense of deceit's substance is cheating someone out of something.

This deceit is at the core of this deception. Satan defrauded Adam by corrupting Eve, using the tree of knowledge of good and evil and God's command to Adam. So many attempts are made to defraud Christians out of their support stemming from scripture and the bridge of faith in what is written within it. Then it needs to be replaced with something else. This is at the core of deceiving a person, the taking of Jesus from their preview. The attempts by unbelievers at calling the Bible flawed, inadequate, ineffective, or requiring an update to it to reflect today's standards of behavior are nothing new. Nothing is new to the standards of life for the unbeliever. However, it is the present-day deception. Jacob used the actions of deception and fraud to get what he wanted from Esau and Isaac. This type of behavior still goes on today in religious systems and within everyday life.

Another documented deception involved the sons of Jacob. The psalmist wrote, "My enemies are lively; they are strong; and my haters increase by deception."[131] The sons of Jacob created the conditions of deliberate harm to Shechem and Hamor, who defiled their sister. They sought revenge through deception in the form of defrauding them. The psalmist wrote, "His mouth is full of cursing and deceit and fraud; under his tongue are mischief and vanity."[132] Job wrote, "They conceive mischief, and bring forth evil, and their belly prepares deceit.[133] These people use words bent on deception, although perceptions adorn them with wisdom and tender care. In the case of the sons of Jacob, this wisdom leads toward revenge and violence.[134] The language of deception filled with evil framing in pleasant words is misleading.[135] In the end, their counsel is nothing more than a falsehood.[136] This imagination of evil for revenge comes from the heart of deceit.[137] It is hatred in pretending and storing up deceit to be manipulative and dominating of others.[138] It is stories like this in which the underlining standards of deception and the smoothing words mistaken for acceptable standards of association with behavior are still sin.

Wages of Sin

> **The wages of sin is death, but the gift of God is eternal life through Jesus Christ our Lord.[139]**

"The wages of sin" means more than just death. Jesus explains this, saying, "He who reaps receives wages and gathers fruit to life eternal, so that both he, who sows and he who reaps may rejoice together."[140] Jesus suggests that, whether the work is sin or righteous, the wages we receive pay off in eternal dividends. However, he also suggests there is an eternal division concerning the righteous and the unrighteous, saying,

> He, who overcomes will inherit all things, and I will be his God, and he will be my son. The fearful, and the unbelieving, and the abominable, and murders, and whoremongers, and sorcerers, and idolaters, and all liars, will have their part in the Lake burning with fire and brimstone, which is the second death.[141]

It suggests a torment for eternity and a severed relationship with God. It is living godlessly based on your own terms without God's help for all eternity; that is the point. This is a horrible condition as unrighteousness in whatever minimal amount, with sin's acceptability, leads to a second death for eternity. The other possibility is to be a part of God's family, where Jesus's father is our father. He is the one taking care of us for all eternity, with us as his children. This suggests more than just the mere death of our bodies and then peace; it suggests either eternal separation from God or being his children.

A resurrection will occur before the great judgment. These people participating in the resurrection have a condition over which the "second death has no authority."[142] This results from Christ's intercession for us; as Paul wrote, "It is now having been manifested by the appearing of our savior, Jesus Christ, who has made death of no effect, bringing life and immortality to light through the gospel."[143] The gospel comes from the information provided in the Bible about Jesus, which has an impact on the unbeliever. To reiterate, Paul wrote to the Romans, "So, faith comes by hearing, and hearing by the word of God."[144] It is this great God, Jesus, who "is the Mediator of the new covenant, so, that by means of death, for the redemption of the transgressions that were under the first covenant, those, who are called might receive the promise of eternal life."[145] This eternal inheritance comes from God. It is Jesus who intercedes on our behalf. Our faith, as the finished product of sin's atonement and remission of sin, is through the shedding of his blood for us.

The Lamb's book of life is more than mere names. This book belongs to Jesus, who is the only individual authorized to mark out or put names in it. It is according to his will, not ours. Moses wrote about his experience concerning it, "Now, will you forgive their sin! If not, I pray you blot me out of your book, which you have written. Jehovah said to Moses, whoever has sinned against me, I will blot him out of my book."[146] Although Moses confronted God about his frustration and was told to go back to work, John wrote the consequences of the conditions of sin in a prophetic message as well. He wrote, "If anyone was not found having been written in the Book of Life, he was cast into the Lake of Fire."[147] The term *cast* here has the connotation of someone being violently flung against their will, kicking and screaming while pleading for their life, saying that they are perfectly acceptable based on their own designations and definitions. An everlasting and eternal condition of judgment is placed upon the unbeliever.

No one can take Christ's place. No one will take Christ's place, nor could anyone ever take his place. John wrote of Christ, "I am the First and Last. I am He, who lives, and was dead, and behold, I am alive forevermore. Amen. I have the keys of Hades and of Death."[148] He was recalling Isaiah when Christ, as Jehovah, said, "Thus says the Lord, the King of Israel, and His Redeemer, the Lord of Host: 'I am the First and I am the Last; besides me there is no God [elohiym]."[149] This great Jehovah qualifies himself: "Listen to me, O Jacob, and Israel, whom I called! I am he; I am the first and I am the last. My hand laid the foundation of the earth, and my right hand spread out the heavens; when I call to them, they stand forth together."[150] This makes Christ not only the creator of the universe and all that is in it but also God of all the humanity. Even the psalmist knew this issue was God's alone, writing, "Our God is the God of salvation; and to Jehovah are the issues of death."[151] The resulting condition of death for the believer "is now having been manifested by the appearing of our Savior Jesus Christ, who has made death of no effect, bringing life and immortality to light through the gospel."[152] This suggests a better way of life. This gospel of Jesus comes from the scripture, and the scripture is the foundation of the trust and the faith we have in Christ to do his job of atonement for the remission of our sins and providing our names to be written in his book of life.

Consequences of Sin

> **They are cursed children, who have forsaken the right way and have gone astray, following the way of Balaam, the son of Beor, who loved the wages of unrighteousness, but had reproof of his lawbreaking, a dumb ass speaking in a man's voice, held back the madness of the prophet.[153]**

The consequence of sin is death. Dying by sin is slow and painful, while God seeks to save sinners through his mercy and grace[154] through repentance. Of course, the acceptance of God's gift of salvation involves repentance. God desires all humans' salvation and for them not to perish[155] due to their unhealable, unrestorable, sinful condition. This sinful condition comes to us through Adam's disobeying the order of Christ concerning not eating the fruit of the tree of knowledge of good and evil. This is when death passed to all humankind and the world. People's behavior will condemn them when facing the final judgment. God required Ezekiel to speak for him, as he wrote, "As I live, says the Lord Jehovah, I have no delight in the death of the wicked, except in the turning of the wicked from his way, and so, to live. Turn, turn from your evil ways; for why will you die?"[156] Jesus's concern is the desire for everyone to come to repentance and thus heal their relationships with the Father of heaven. Death due to sinful practice is not a desire of God, the Father of heaven, or Christ.

The sinful condition leads unbelievers to believe the lie. Unbelievers accept anything other than the mercy of God's grace toward them. This is when they are bound to this slavery of sin. God reiterates his position: "I have no delight in the death of him who dies, says the Lord Jehovah. Therefore, turn and live."[157] Repentance is a required action formulated from God's statements. Without repentance, sin is laid to our account and is without relief or reprieve.

The acceptance of Christ's atonement for the remission of sin requires judgment upon our action by God's grace and mercy toward us. Jesus has completed his task against sin, with "the last enemy made to cease is death."[158] It is Christ who can make the statement as God, "I will ransom them from the power of the grave; I will redeem them from death. O Death, where are your plagues; O Grave, where is your ruin!"[159] It was Christ, our redeemer, who is our redeemer from this death of sin—thus, "Death is through man, the resurrection of the dead also is through a man. For as in Adam all die, even so in Christ all will be made alive."[160] Although the lack of repentance causes us to be carnally minded, "carnally minded is death, but to be spiritually minded is life and peace."[161] "Christ Jesus has made [us] free from the law of sin and death."[162] The final measurement for sin written by Paul states, "The wages of sin is death, but the gift of God is eternal life through Jesus Christ, our Lord."[163] "We had the sentence of death in ourselves, so, that we should not trust ourselves."[164] "The gift of righteousness shall reign in life by One, Jesus Christ."[165] The slow dying from sin is a grievous rejection of Christ's permanent atonement for sin.

Future of Sin

> **He must have suffered often since the foundation of the world, but now, once in the end of the world He has appeared to put away sin by sacrifice of Himself. As it is appointed to men once to die, but after this, the judgment, so, Christ was once offered to bear the sins of many. To those who look for him He shall appear the second time without sin to salvation.[166]**

Judgment for sin is coming. Daniel saw this in his explicit and unfulfilled prophesy. As he wrote, "Seventy weeks are decreed as to your people and as to your holy city, to finish the transgression and to make an end of sins, and to make atonement for iniquity, and to bring in everlasting righteousness, and to seal up the vision and prophecy, and to anoint the Most Holy."[167] This end of sin and transgression spoken of in detail in Revelation is the timeline of things still coming. Paul continues, "He is bringing the matter to an end, cutting short in righteousness, because the Lord will make short work on the earth."[168] A finality is determined for sin in heaven and required upon all during the day of judgment.

We will stand before Christ. For all, there will be a reckoning, a holding to account, for our actions by judgment. Then we will be met with a decree of reward as good stewards or with eternal separation. The finality includes deceivers and the deception from liars, with "their part [is] the Lake burning with fire and brimstone, which is the second death."[169] This is the requirement of repentance leading toward salvation, while sin is running rampant. Judgment demands an end to sin and transgressions through either our death or the atonement by Jesus through repentance. Judgment will end in permanency based on our personal condition and position with Jesus.

The issue is escaping our own required death consequences for sin. The writer of Hebrews declares to us,

For if the word spoken through angels proved steadfast, and every transgression and disobedience received a just reward, how shall we escape if we neglect so great a salvation, which at first began to be spoken by the Lord, and was confirmed to us by those, who heard him, God also, bearing witness both with signs and wonders, with various miracles, and gifts of the Holy Spirit, according to His will.[170]

No one has fallen so far that Christ cannot save them. The great God of creation, this holy and righteous God, first took on human form.[171] He stripped himself of all his power and reputation and was humble and obedient for the atonement by blood on the cross for us all. "For we do not have a High Priest, who cannot sympathize with our weaknesses, but was in all points tempted as we are, yet without sin,"[172] and yet, "He made Him, who knew no sin to be sin for us that we might become the righteousness of God in him."[173] As Christ hung on that cursed tree, he experienced the terrible rejection of God, being sin for us, and he spoke out, "My God, My God, why have you forsaken me?"[174, 175] No person has fallen so far as Christ, in that Christ's atonement of blood cannot clear our need of the remission of our sins.

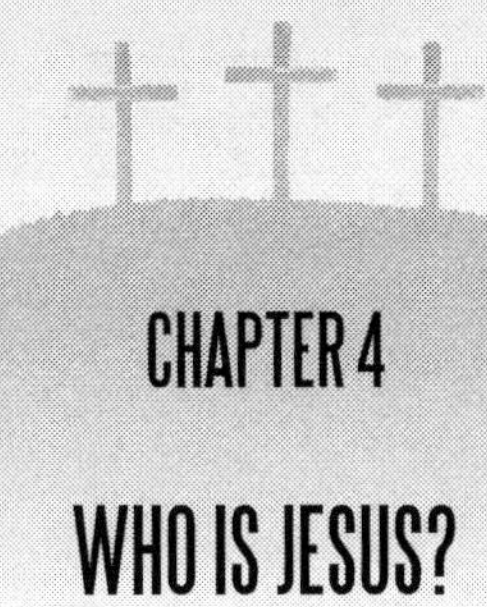

CHAPTER 4

WHO IS JESUS?

For your Maker is your husband, the LORD of host is his name; and your redeemer is the Holy One of Israel; he is called the God of the whole earth.[176]

The discussion of Christ reveals a vast number of thoughts concerning him. Some have said he is a prophet, while others say he is a great or good man. In our world today, Christ's being written out of the picture is the norm as he is rejected in many areas of life. In philosophy classes, this great and profound philosopher is not found in the books and his impact is forgotten. The schools are void of him, and Christians are condemned for even talking about Jesus or his existence. On the other hand, Satan has made all things under heaven the idols and gods that people worship today. "Who is Jesus?" seems to be the most important question to answer.

This original question Jesus asked seems appropriate. Christ asked his disciples, "Who do you say that I am?"[177] Even though Christ asked this question in his time, it makes each of us even today decide the issue. In settling the question concerning Jesus Christ, we are seeking a conclusion of Christ's statement concerning who he is in our lives. Deciding Christ's place in our lives is the only real requirement for all of us in life. This is the only real question we need to answer for ourselves. For example, David wrote a song praising God for his marvelous works,[178] and when Jesus healed the blind man, the blind man was held accountable for worshipping him.[179] This Jesus is the God of creation,[180, 181] and this Jehovah Elohiym who controls all qualifies himself, saying, "I am Jehovah, and there is none else, no God beside me."[182] In fact, this great God of creation goes farther, saying, "Therefore, know this day, and consider it in your heart, that the Lord, Himself, is God in heaven above and on the earth beneath; there is no other."[183] Jesus is God, the Jehovah Elohiym.

This Christ is the great God Jehovah. God made signs and wonders so "that you might know that the Lord Himself is God, there is none other besides Him."[184] This is for all humankind's benefit, for God wants that "all the people of the earth may know that the Lord is God; there is no other. Let your heart therefore be loyal to the Lord, our God, to walk in His statutes and keep His commandments."[185] Daniel knew about this connection between God and prophecy when he sought God to reveal the secret of Nebuchadnezzar, knowing God "reveals the deep and secret things."[186] Nebuchadnezzar's response to Daniel, as told by Daniel, was, "Truly your God is the God of gods, the Lord of kings, and a revealer of secrets, since you could reveal this secret."[187] Nebuchadnezzar went on to write,

> The end of the time I, Nebuchadnezzar, lifted my eyes to heaven, and my understanding returned to me; and I blessed the Most High and praised and honored Him, who lives forever: for His dominion is an everlasting dominion, and His kingdom is from generation to generation. All the inhabitants of the earth are reputed as nothing; He does according to His will in the army of heaven and among the inhabitants of the earth. No one can restrain His hand or say to Him, "What have you done?" … Now, I Nebuchadnezzar, praise and extol and honor the King of heaven, all of whose works are truth, and His ways justice.[188]

Nebuchadnezzar appears to have had a prophetic moment in recognizing Jesus as the God of gods. This nonbeliever of God made a prophetic statement like Ezekiel's prophecy, as a convert, a neonate in Christendom with Jesus as the Jehovah Elohiym. John in Revelation then confirms the prophetic message of this Jesus in full detail as the God of gods.

The point is this: Jesus is the God of creation, who is the Christ of heaven and earth. Jesus is the God of prophecy, and he is the one worthy of our taking notice. This Jesus is the God of our salvation, and through none other is there a provision of atonement for salvation for the human condition.

Christ's Status before Being Human

Christ is the Jehovah of hosts, the Lord of armies. The term *Jehovah God* (Jehovah Elohiym), used for the creator of creation in Genesis 2:4, is just one of his accolades. This preeminence of Christ, according to Paul, was a reference to this Jehovah Elohiym of Genesis who created the world, humankind, and all that is in heaven. He is the one who formed man out of the dust of the ground.[189] This is paramount not only to history but to everyone today. The seraphs call him the Jehovah of hosts.[190] Jesus was the maker of all things.[191] Although "The Lord your God is a consuming fire, a jealous God,[192]" he qualifies himself, saying, "I, the Lord, am the first and with the last; I am he."[193] Jesus goes on to say through Isaiah, "Jehovah, the king of Israel, and His redeemer, Jehovah of Host; I am the first and the last; and besides me there is no God."[194] Finally, Christ qualifies himself in Revelation, saying, "I am the Alpha and Omega, the Beginning and the Ending, the First and the Last."[195] Jesus is the Jehovah God.

It is not good enough to qualify yourself as a god. The world accepts many gods, but because they define their own lives through the world's designed qualification, it is still false. This state is unhealthy. It was the Jehovah Elohiym who "formed man of the dust of the ground, and breathed into his nostrils the breath of life;

and man [Adam] became a living soul."[196] While making the best of our lives with the choices we make, it is not good enough to be gods of our own making. It was Christ, who created all things for himself and for his own purposes. He is the "stone for a foundation, a tried stone, a precious cornerstone, a sure foundation."[197] Whereas others attempt to qualify you as a willing participant for an ascended position of godhood, it is God who determines who will face fire in the last judgment. It was this Christ who was praying for the restoration of his former glory with his father.[198] It is this Jesus Christ who is "our Redeemer, Jehovah of Host is His name, the Holy One of Israel."[199] Although our best efforts will never be good enough to meet God's requirements, Jesus is qualified for the position, being God and mediator for us all.

Reason for Christ's Humanity

> **Come now, and let us reason together, says Jehovah; though your sins are as scarlet, they shall be as white as snow; though they are red like crimson, they shall be like wool.[200]**

Humans are always looking for innocence in their lives. However, in the *Christian Study Bible*, the above verse reads, "Come let us settle the question," which brings the issue of the human condition to a point of conclusion. When people choose to promote their chosen dysfunctions of sin as being healthy and acceptable, they are still engaged in sinful acts. The corruption of sin tarnishes our souls. When we look at ourselves, we see the blackness of our shame and our guilt strangling us. We try to work ourselves into God's good graces by doing good and thus find ourselves in a poor situation for meeting God on his terms and standards. We are never at peace with ourselves or others. We can never reach God's good graces on our own merits or through our human limitations. Our lives, qualified by God's standards, are lacking when measured against

God's holiness. Christ fills our lack of God's holiness, righteousness, and peace.

Christ came to provide a means for humankind to receive the remission of sins. He humbled himself, becoming obedient to death on a cross for the atonement required for our sin. The judgment required for our sin was a result of our own chosen behaviors[201] that became flagrant. For this reason, Christ's humanity was to put an end to our transgressions and our sins, make a permanent payment of atonement for the iniquity impugned to us, and bring an everlasting righteousness.[202] He stripped himself of his glory and, as the Jehovah Elohiym, made himself of no reputation in servitude to the Father for the purpose of our salvation. Because of Christ, there is no work we can do to make our way into God's good graces for our salvation.

Christ changes everything due to sin's infection. During the moment of communion with his disciples, he states his new covenant: "My blood of the new covenant, which is shed for many for the remission of sin."[203] It is for this reason Christ can say, "Their sin and their iniquities, I will remember no more. Where remission of these, there is no more offering for sin."[204] He finished the process that was needed for the redemption from sin to be complete. However, without him, we are all most miserable[205] people because of our inability to be at peace with our sinful selves. It was Christ who "delivered us from the power of darkness."[206] It is this Jesus of Nazareth "in whom we have redemption through his blood, the remission of sins."[207] Redemption from the impact of sin comes only through Christ's atonement of blood on the cross.

Salvation comes as a permanent status of Christ. John the Baptist, the forerunner of Jesus, came baptizing people and preaching repentance and baptism for the remission of sin, to prepare the people's hearts and share knowledge of the coming salvation[208] through Christ. John the Baptist was talking about Jesus Christ when he said to behold the "Lamb of God, who takes away the sin of the world."[209] Peter said about Christ, "The one God has exalted to be a ruler and savior to His right hand in order to give repentance and remission of sins to Israel."[210] Yet this salvation extends to Gentiles as well. Thus, the expansion of children of faith's salvation to you and to me is due to the permanency of Christ's status.

Jesus Christ has become the high priest. This requires us to draw near to him "with a true heart in full assurance of faith … without wavering."[211] Christ, having entered the Holy of Holies, which was not made with human hands, appeared to put away sin through his sacrifice for the last time.[212] Peter says of Jesus "that it is he, who was ordained of God to be the judge of the living and the dead. All the prophets give witness to him that through his name, whoever believes in him shall receive the remission of sins."[213] In addition, we are to provoke one another to love and do good works, assembling ourselves together and exhorting one another until the day approaches. We are to live out our salvation with the grace and love given us. It is Christ who assures us of the permanent status of the remission of our sin through the atonement of his blood for us on the cross as he mediates as high priest for us today.

Purpose of Emmanuel among Us

> **For God is one, and there is one Mediator of God and of men, the Man, Christ Jesus, who gave Himself a ransom for all, to be testified in due time.[214]**

Christ is Immanuel among us. His name means "God with us." He comes from a virgin bride who conceived by unnatural means to give birth to a male child miraculously.[215] Since she knew no man,[216] this is an impossible feat by today's standards of DNA knowledge. The miraculous nature of Christ's life truly is God among us.

The eternal purpose of Christ was to bring us into the mystery of the fellowship with God. Yet Jesus said of himself, "Do not think that I have come to destroy the law or the prophets. I have not come to destroy, but to fulfill."[217] Who then is this Jesus, this Christ, who created all things,[218] and this God of creation, who walked with Adam and Eve face to face in the garden? We are under the care of this Christ, who is the author and finisher of our faith.[219] The prophecies of Christ state that he is God, with no other like him. His declarations define a beginning and an end and do his pleasure.[220] "Christ, the head of all things in heaven and earth, has purposed a predestination of inheritance according to the counsel of His own will."[221] Jesus came to undo the impact and practices of sin and the works of Satan.[222] Christ has come to bring us into fellowship with his Father by destroying the impact of Satan's deception and manifesto on humanity through the righteousness of faith in his atonement for our sins.

The lonely lie the world tells us is that all things are good. This lie comes from a misinterpretation of a statement Paul made to the Romans: "We know that all things work together for good, to those who love God, to those who are called according to his purpose."[223] In the world, where people go to great lengths to hide their works and purposes from God, this woe of sin comes with a debt always needing payment.[224] Christ's death puts an end to Satan's power, discredits and removes his manifesto from our lives, and retains the right for him to judge all people and all things. This is where the remarkable handiwork of Satan's manifesto and his deception are used to enslave us to the law and to restrain us from Christ. However, the law's design drives us to Christ. Christ changes everything by changing the equation with faith, salvation, restitution, restoration, and remission of sin by the atonement of blood—his blood.

Final Judge for All

> **Therefore, I solemnly witness before God and the Lord Jesus Christ, who is going to judge the living and the dead according to His appearance and His kingdom.[225]**

Judgment is coming for us all. Even Christians have trouble with this concept. No one cares to have their choices and decisions critiqued as being either good or evil. Their choices are their own, and no one wants to be judged for their chosen actions. No person likes to pay consequences for their decisions or involvement in behavior that is accountable for a pending judgment. However, some go so far as to create an arena of having a God with no judgment. Then they extend this lack of judgment to imagine the condemnation of people into an eternity *without* a tormented expulsion from God. Thus, there is no hell, no eternal punishment, and no presiding God over us all, and Jesus is nothing more than a figment of some poor soul's imagination. Others think that hell is on earth, right here and right now, and there is no real hell. Some think the church is the best of conditions. Others idolize the church as being more important than Christ or more important than the atonement he provides for their sins. Many do not like this news of a coming judgment; thus, they attempt to write God out of the picture, as if he never existed. Like Satan, they depreciate Christ into a form of uselessness and idolatry. As the writer of Hebrews wrote, "It is appointed to men once to die, but after this the judgment,"[226] suggesting that there is judgment for all after this life—both for living in evil or for doing good. Judgment is discredited by some who do not believe in a torment apart from God for eternity. However, judgment comes for us all.

We have no power in changing God's decisions about us. The adding or removing of our names from the Lamb's book of life indicates that we have no power to alter it. It does not matter if you were a good person, for if your name is not found in the Lamb's book of life, there is only one result. This result is "each one of them was judge according to their works."[227] Paul wrote to the Corinthians concerning this issue: "We must all appear before the judgment seat of Christ, so that each one may receive the things done though the body, according to that which he has done, whether good or bad."[228] John wrote about the significance of this book of the Lamb in Revelation: "I saw the dead, the small and great, stand before God. Books were opened, and another book was opened, which is the Book of Life. The dead were judged out of those things, which were written in the books, according to their works."[229] It was Moses who was contending with Christ out of his frustration and anger while working as the mediator between Christ and the Israelites. He asked Christ to blot out his name from his book,[230] but Christ told him it was none of his business. This book of life makes a huge difference for people not found in it, as written: "If anyone was not found being written in the Book of Life, he was cast into the Lake of Fire."[231] However, this term *cast,* meaning to throw with a violent flinging, against your will, kicking, screaming, and pleading for your life into the lake of fire, is a condition all but forgotten. It refers to a place of permanent judgment in the separation between the unbeliever and God for eternity. The Lamb's book of life is Christ's responsibility alone; he marks out or writes people's names into his book. It is associated with the acceptance of the free gift of salvation from the offer of atonement by blood on the cross for the remission of sin.

CHAPTER 5

JESUS MAKES ALL THE DIFFERENCE

The sorrows of hell hemmed me in. The snares of death went in front of me.[232]

There is a question of grave importance: What is the difference made by Christ? This seems like a very logical and reasonable question. The depreciation of this question, the concern about Jesus in the world's ignorance, and the world's contempt in disbelief concerning Christ ends with the answer to this question being in obscurity. The graveness of this question results in the same consequence of Adam's disobedience of Christ in the garden. There is a required holding place for people of sin that holds them accountable for the responsibilities that require consequences and punishment. There is a paradise for those who choose faith and a place of torment of hell for the unbelievers.[233] The story of the rich man and Lazarus told by Christ is a true account because he shares private knowledge and does not qualify it as parable. However, in final judgment, death and hell are cast into the Lake of Fire, where the torment of eternity goes on forever. Not being in the Lamb's book of life causes a person's violent casting into the lake of fire to be tormented for all eternity. For "this is the second death."[234] The consequences of rejecting Christ lead to sin, disbelief, and the blotting out of a name in the Lamb's book of life.

Christ makes the difference in eternity. He qualifies himself, saying, "I am the First and the Last, the Living One, I became dead, and behold, I am alive for ever and ever, Amen. I have the keys of hell and of death."[235] Hell is a scary place, "so, hell has enlarged itself, and opened its mouth without measure; their glory, their multitude, their pride, and he, who rejoices in her, shall go down into it. Jehovah of Host is exalted in judgment, and God, the Holy One is sanctified in righteousness."[236] Hell is designed for Satan and those who follow him; they "shall be brought down to hell, to the sides of the pit."[237] Satan and the angels that followed him are "kept in everlasting chains under darkness for the judgment of a great Day."[238] It was Christ who made the final touch to this scenario, saying, "Do not fear those who kill the body, but are not able to kill the soul. Rather fear him who can destroy both the soul and the body in hell."[239] Christ, being God, has the final say upon the judgment of humankind and the angels he created.

The tongue used for lifting Christ up draws people to him. Christ did not waste words on people teaching hypocrisy, such as the scribes and Pharisees. James wrote of the tongue and its power in life, "The tongue is a fire, a world of iniquity. So, the tongue is set among our members, spotting all the body, and inflaming the course of nature, and inflamed by hell."[240] While the teachers of the Jewish community sought for a single proselyte, and in teaching this neonate their religious practices, they then became twice the hypocrite and child of hell than themselves.[241] Teaching is the use of the tongue to guide people to or from Christ.

Today, deception is on the rampage. It discredits Christ with the dishonesty in disqualifying the truth of scriptures and invalidating righteousness through it. It discredits Christ by disposing him from his position of the Son of God and the procreator of salvation. It disqualifies the truth of the scriptures by attempting to rewrite the scripture to suit the person's chosen deviance in life. It invalidates righteousness by bringing the level of godhood down to our own chosen morality. This same quality of deceptive teaching fires up the new neonate to carry on the nature of deception with all the passion of ignorance and innocence. The tongue truly becomes an "unruly evil, full of deathly poison."[242] The corrupted tongue spreads its deception among the innocent and isolated and fills the void with an ignorance of Christ. It spreads an inadequate knowledge of Christ caused by the lack of the scripture's reference, ceasing the search for an answer in Christ.

Impossible State of Man's Sinfulness

> **The way of the fool is right in his own eyes, but he who heeds counsel is wise.[243]**

The state of man's sinfulness has an impossible restitution for repairing the relationship with God. In fact, God spoke of man's heart, saying, "The heart is deceitful above all things, and desperately wicked; who can know it?"[244] Job understood his condition in life, as revealed when he said, "My soul is weary; I will leave my complaint on myself; I will speak in the bitterness of my soul. I will say to God do not condemn me; make me know why you contend with me."[245] For a man or woman in the pains of sorrow bound by sin, this is a great statement for anyone wanting to have peace with God. However, we do not look at ourselves through the eyes of God, and we attempt to justify our lives by our own defined terms and defense.

We are the unwitting ones. We expect to clear our names with God on our own terms and by our own merits. The only problem with this is that we must meet God's terms. The proverb states that there are "many purposes in a man's heart, but the counsel of Jehovah shall stand."[246] Although we desire to remove him from the equation of judgment, we face him anyway. Man's double-mindedness in his heart breeds a life requiring God's judgment upon us. This form of self-imposed crisis demands our need for Christ's atonement for us. Humankind forms a corrupted set of feelings, pleasure, and standards in life and then follows them. Without the scripture as a foundation, without a relationship with Christ, we have no means of straightening our lives toward a right way and a healthy relationship with God. This warps our ways, leading us away from righteous decisions, holy behavior, and a true relationship with Christ as our sovereign.

This self-deception is an evil practice. It writes God out of the picture and removes him from daily life. God knew this when he examined man before the flood, when he saw "that the wickedness of man was great in the earth, and every imagination of the thoughts of his heart was only evil continually."[247] It is this self-defined condition combined with the desire to remove God from our lives and qualifying our actions according to our own standards that leads to sinful behavior. In addition, even after God destroyed humankind, "Jehovah said in his heart, I will never again curse the ground for man's sake, because the imagination of man's heart is evil from his youth."[248] Although we attempt to look good in our own eyes, deception is the vileness of our world.

History repeats itself. Knowing the imaginations of men, Paul wrote to Titus, "Avoid foolish disputes, genealogies, contentions, and strivings about the law; for they are unprofitable and useless. Reject a divisive man after the first and second admonition, knowing that such a person is warped and sinning, begin self-condemned."[249] Paul continued this theme when he wrote to the Romans, "Those who are self-seeking, and do not obey the truth, but obey unrighteousness—indignation and wrath, tribulation and anguish, on every soul of man, who does evil."[250] By adopting Satan's manifesto of being God's equal, we create our own standards, put our blinders on, spit in God's eye, and write Christ out of our lives while kicking him to the curb.

Foolish questions lead to foolish actions. One of these foolish actions is exchanging the Bible for anything else. Another foolish action is questioning the authority of Christ in exchange for idolizing a church over the validity and character of God. Replacing Christ with something less than what he claims is not only foolish but ignorant. Accepting anything as a replacement for Christ is foolish, contradicts the Bible, and has grave consequences. It is nothing more than deceptive sleight of hand, a form of manipulative interaction. Job knew his condition in life and wrote about his feelings of condemnation, bitterness, and contention as he made proclamations of his personal justification.[251] Yet, later, Job had to answer God's questions about his limitations, a scary proposition for anyone facing God on his terms. Paul wrote to the Colossians, "Indeed, having an appearance of wisdom in self-imposed religion, false humility, and neglect of the body, but are of no value against the indulgence of the flesh."[252] The foolishness of the question leads to telling God how to run the world, how to make things happen, and how to live up to our expectations, which we have implemented above God's for our own pleasured satisfaction.

Sin leads to breaking God's commands. This results in the knowledge of sin, death of hope, shame of behavior, and guilt from the violations against this great God who loves us. Solomon wrote, "He who keeps his command will experience nothing harmful; and a wise man's heart discerns both time and judgment."[253] We attempt to write God out of the picture, raising ourselves to the level of godhood. Thus, we can rise to the occasion, and yet, our own actions will condemn us.

Sin does not make us righteous. This is a strange concept in a world that accepts progressive Christianity. However, the issues are self-justification, self-qualification in relativism, and self-defining concerns of what is evil or good. Paul wrote to the Romans,

For what the law could not do in that it was weak through the flesh, God did by sending His own Son in the likeness of sinful flesh, on account of sin: he condemned sin in the flesh, that the righteousness requirement of law might be fulfilled in us who do not walk according to the flesh, but according to the Spirit.[254]

Our righteousness is not by the law. Sin manifested by the law reveals to us our limitations, our sinful nature, and our inability to meet God on his terms. This results in our shamed human condition of limitations, weakness, and inadequacies. We scramble to be something we are not. It is for these reasons that we are corrupted, dysfunctional, and lacking freedom from our sin. Our attempts at raising ourselves into positions of authority over God and dominating others for status, power, and prestige are our downfall. However, the consequence for this rudeness toward Christ has the flavor of contemptuous shame. Christ said, "Therefore, whoever shall be ashamed of Me and My words in this adulterous and sinful generation, the Son of Man shall also be ashamed of him when He comes in the glory of His Father with the Holy Angels."[255] We are inadequate to meet a holy God on righteous terms without Christ as a mediator between us and his Father.

Humankind's sinful character manifests in behavior. The first behavioral act comes in the form of death, and this death is upon all the earth. Sometimes, this comes as a slow dying through our lust and obsessions, but all the same, there is 100 percent certainty that death comes to us all. Paul knew this when he wrote to the Romans,

Therefore, the law is holy, and the commandment holy and just and good. Has then what is good become death to me? Certainly not! But sin, that it might appear sin, was producing death in me through what is good, so that sin through the commandment might become exceedingly sinful.[256]

The law shows us the nature of our sin. It shows us the depth of our attempts to bypass the consequences of our sin. In writing to Timothy, Paul made a list of human behavior characteristics of the last days, knowing it was a grievous time and at hand.[257] This cost of our lives through time, this list, is a set of prophetic behaviors of sin now facing our world that is taking us away from Christ. These sinful behaviors come with the mark of death of our morality, our emotions, our relationships, our sensitivities, and our own lives.

The unrelenting condition of our actions has consequences. Self-control is an exercise of self-restraint,[258] coming in the form of consistent moral integrity.[259] Without self-control, we have powerless lives. A lack of self-control combined with changeable morality cause us to live lives of deception. With a loss in control or restraint of actions, willpower, level-headedness, emotions, reactions, desires, or self-discipline, we fall into sinful behavior and practices. The augmentation of sin in our nature has proven to be an effective foe against our submission to Christ as God in our lives.

The Sin of Self-Love

The first of these behavioral characteristics is self-love. A narcissistic love of self distracts us from the love of God for us. It deprives us of the focus upon Christ, and this lack of focus on Christ's love for us—evident in his death on the cross for our sin—is a rejection of him. Self-love is a fondness of the self[260] that is a baffling and backward[261] form of love focused on the self. It is an overt attempt at being a friend, associate, or neighbor[262] to ourselves, forgetting the commands of Christ to love one another. The sin of self-love is driven by self-preservation, which is the promotion of our own welfare and well-being with excessive regard for our own advantage.

It is hard to think in terms of Christ. Christ stated, "He, who loves his life will lose it, and he who hates his life in this world will keep it for eternal life."[263] The conceit and vanity of self-love has become the standard of today's morality. We think of our standards overshadowing God's as our contrived religious traditions, which have become the traditions of humankind. We lose our relationship with God and Christ in the mix. In many religious systems, we further the church's instructions without question, succumbing to our own ignorance of the scripture. The result is that self-love becomes our false teacher. We consider self-love as perfectly holy, acceptable, and accurate, while excusing God with our active engagement with the sinful practice as it takes us away from Christ.

The Sin of the Love of Money

Lovers of money come in a close second in the race of ungodly behavior. This is the foundation for the character traits of avarice, greed, and covetousness. Loving money is a pathological condition of keeping things to ourselves to have an edge over others. It has an affiliation with stinginess, causing our compassion for others to be nil. It includes the illicit desire for power, property, and prestige in an aggressive, predatory, insatiable, and unprincipled manner. The writer of Hebrews wrote, "Let your way of life be without the love of money and be content with such things as you have."[264] This removes the covetousness of wanting more compared to others.

This is extremely hard in a world promoting that we need more than what we have. The world wants to make us better than what we are. Paul writes to Timothy, "For the love of money is a root of all evils, of which some having lusted after, they were seduced from the faith and pierced themselves through with many sorrows."[265] The greed of making more money, having more possessions, or gaining an advantage due to our presentation of wealth is an ongoing issue of caste and prejudice. Although we see the major error of this in everyday life, the love of money is an evil desire to have control over others, usurping Christ in our lives to do it.

We never think of a love of money as being an attempt to be God's equal. We take his authority on for ourselves and, with it, demonstrate our affluence in front of other people. This prestige is an overt identity of superiority and authority of control over others. In addition, we do not think of not justifying God as evidence of a love of money. However, it is a love of God's position, the power in controlling the money, prestige, and property for our own purposes, that drives our love of his authority and our idolatry in life. We are faced with God's alternative for us, as Isaiah wrote, "Ho! Everyone who thirsts, come to the waters; and you who has no money, come, buy, and eat. Yea, come, buy wine, milk without money and without price."[266] This is a gift of God's grace bestowed on the individual in exchange for attempting to be God's equal.

We are beings with limitations. The foundation of our nature is sin, and we are broken from this sin. With Christ in our lives, we have the freedom to come into God's presence without price. We can come and, without money, eat and drink freely from God's good graces. When Christ talked about hungering and thirsting after righteousness,[267] he said,

They shall neither hunger anymore, nor thirst anymore; the sun shall not strike them, nor any heat for the Lamb, who is in the midst of the throne will shepherd them and lead them to living fountains of waters, and God will wipe away every tear from their eyes.[268]

This is an explicit prophetic message about believers coming from the tribulation of judgment and being allowed into the realm of God's home forever. Our lust for God's position is exchanged for access to people's faith in us, allowing them to succumb to our manipulation through their submission and taking away God's property. This is the love of money.

The Sin of Boasting

Boasting is the sin of bragging. It is vaunting and lifting ourselves, wishing and praying for better form, in the form of embellished gloating. It is the process of patting ourselves on the back and blowing our own horns in celebration when there is nothing to celebrate. It is a foolish celebration of self. Boasting is the shining personal show of a rave in a moment of being better than everyone else. This superiority is better than Christ in our lives. It is the ornamentation and brilliance of being right in one's own eyes. This is the nature of the sin of boasting; the formulation of bragging lies with a boasting self-glory.

Boasting is the prejudice of contempt for everything other than ourselves. It involves comparing our own experiences to those of someone else. We see this great pleasure of self-indulgence from Satan when his pride attempted to boost him to the level of godhood[269] and culminates in the pits of hell. It is a crippling and thwarting impedance of equality that triggers complaints about God's or Christ's not being a respecter of persons. Boasting fills life with an unsound and illegal responsibility of authority or superiority. James suggested to us, "Now you boast in your presumptions. All such boasting is evil."[270] Boasting leads us to Job's sin, which was being righteous in his own eyes. This is perfectly OK and acceptable in our world today. However, Job's issue was due to his justifying himself rather than God.[271] Justifying ourselves is boasting from the prejudice of a falsehood of real superiority.

Sin is a means of boasting. It dishonors God, discredits the need for Christ, and breaks the law by creating its own qualifications for the law.[272] If I boast, the issue is not that I am justifying myself; it is that I am being foolish about the truth. The boasting is not qualified through the written standards of God or the demands for Christ's atonement for sin. Yet the scripture provides valid requirements for the exposure of God's authority and allows Christ to be effective in our lives.[273] The final tally for boasting is in a faith that saves. Paul wrote to the Ephesians, "For by grace are you saved through faith, and that not of yourselves, it is a gift of God, not of works, lest anyone should boast."[274] The sin of boasting reflects the ridiculous absurdity and futility of self. It is the ineffectual degrading and frustrating proof of the self as better than God. We attempt this by blowing our own horns to prove we do not need Christ in our lives.

The Sin of Pride

Pride is the worst work of sin. Pride is an arrogant ornament of seething insolence, teeming with grandeur. It is a rising and mounting majestic air of superiority or authority and a soaring elation or loftiness that has an insolence to it and emboldens us to acts of exaltation. It is normally importunate in its bulwark of vaulting ourselves. Pride captures the subject with boasting, a quality and condition of strutting and haughtiness. This haughtiness appears to be conspicuously above and beyond the show of superiority. This is the true nature of prejudice appearing as the sin of pride.

There are lots of examples of pride. Samuel learned about pride when the family of King David was so vain toward their younger, weaker brother, when he said, "I know your pride and the naughtiness of your heart."[275] In addition, scripture says of pride, "Therefore, pride enchains them; violence covers them like a robe."[276] The conditions of pride lead us to destruction, as written: "pride comes, then shame comes."[277] John understood this condition of sin when he wrote, "All that is in the world, the lust of the flesh, the lust of the eyes, and the pride of life, is not of the father, but is of the world."[278] Pride is an arrogant, deceiving slave driver about which Obadiah wrote, "The pride of your heart has deceived you."[279] Job knew about the state of pride and discussed its relationship with God, writing, "God will not withdraw his anger; the helpers of pride stoop under him."[280] Furthermore, Job called others the "sons of pride [or whelps]."[281] Pride hides in secrecy, plotting the strife of the tongue, and takes shelter from the scrutiny of God.[282] God will not listen to the prayers from the evil of pride, as Job attested, "There they cry, but he gives no answer, because of the pride of evil doers."[283] In addition, "pride goes before destruction, and a haughty spirit before a fall."[284] "The fear of Jehovah is to hate evil; I hate pride, and arrogance, and the evil, and the wicked mouth,"[285] which pride brings to our world. Pride deceives us in making ourselves better in our own eyes when under the scrutiny of or in subjugation to God and his standards.

The Sin of Blaspheming

Blasphemers are those who vilify Christ. What comes through rumors and alterations is blasphemy, but Christ is what life needs. This impious vilification of Christ is a grossly obscene abuse at Christ's expense. This defamatory action is the deficiency of veneration or respect toward God. Christ spoke of the blasphemy of the Holy Spirit as the gravest of sin. He said, "All sins shall be forgiven to the sons of men, and blasphemies with which they shall blaspheme. He who blasphemes against the Holy Spirit never shall have forgiveness but is liable to eternal condemnation [danger of eternal damnation]."[286, 287, 288] It is an insulting offense, sometimes vulgar, sometimes of sweet deception, that lacks reverence and abuses the status of God's authority. Ungodly people's lives built from blasphemy are a source of rebellious treason and disloyalty against the God of creation.

Blasphemy hinders the gospel of Jesus. Sin causes the enemies of God to blaspheme.[289] Some speak irreverently against Christ's position as God or the Son of God. This disrespect for Christ's status as atoning savor is rebellious wickedness against him and his status as reigning king, and thus, it is blasphemous. It is the blooming scorn of flashes of slanderous and defamatory speech. Paul says of this condition, "For they changed the truth of God into a lie, and they worshiped and served the created things more than the Creator, who is blessed forever."[290] The extent of blasphemy comes from evil slander and abuse in the form of profanity, cursing, and uttering impieties, which shows a disrespect for God as the divine being or for sacred things from him. Christ spoke of people who say they are holy and righteous children of God but are not: "I know the blasphemy of those saying themselves to be Jews and are not, but are of the synagogue of Satan."[291] We see a prophetic message of blasphemy in Revelation as the dragon gives power to the beast: "It opened its mouth in blasphemy toward God, to blaspheme his name and his tabernacle, and those dwelling in heaven."[292] This is the nature of blasphemy—to give the appearance of holiness and righteousness lifted in arrogant contempt for the things of God. Blasphemy is dishonest and deceptive in impersonating God's condition, people, or standards in an attempt to replace them.

The Sin of Disobedience to Parents

Disobedience began a long time ago. In today's world, disobedience is an ongoing issue of morality. As the family breaks down after responsibility for it has slowly eroded with disobedience to parents, it becomes an aggravated issue. Adam was the first to show humankind's displeasure to God though his sin of disobedience to the command about not eating of the fruit in the garden. The disregard for adherence to God's standards was the sin of disobedience, which put an end to his way of life. Even if we mishear a command or are taught wrongly, this does not save us from the consequences of our disobedience. The sin of disobedience includes attempting to approximate the holiness of God and not being holy in comparison. Disobedience also takes the form of neglecting the scripture.

This lack of obedience is a refusal to comply with Christ. Disobedience disregards the command for atonement for sin, validates the transgression, and assumes the behavior is acceptable. Unbelieving people are dead in their trespasses and sin, and they remain slaves in their disobedience against repentance and acceptance of Christ's atonement. They are under the authority of the prince of the power of the air, who is Satan.[293] These children of disobedience exhibit behaviors that fulfill their lusts and desires and fuel the wants of the flesh, being children of wrath. Some people call this hedonism, others just pleasure, but in God's world it is disobedience and rebellion. However, many times, we consider our behavior to not be bad, wicked, or filled with iniquity. Thus, our belief is that we will not face God in judgment. Disobedience is measured against our need for Christ and his standards of living. In addition, Paul admonishes us, "Let no man deceive you with vain words, for because of these things the wrath of God comes upon the children of disobedience."[294] Disobedience has the consequence of the future wrath of God. It is this point exactly that is the first order of business to remove the power and authority of the scripture and then replace it with something else that does not speak of this wrath coming upon sin. The skepticism regarding God's being in control negates our answering to him.

This is the foundation for the disbelief stemming from disobedience. It is our reluctance to accept the power of the truth within the Bible to change our lives. The children of disobedience behave in ways that run toward "fornication, uncleanness, passion, evil desires, and covetousness (which is idolatry),"[295] bringing the wrath of God toward them. Although we often negate sin and disobedience in minimalistic views, our sin becomes acceptable in its limitations. And yet, it is the sin of disobedience.

If every transgression and disobedience received a just recompense of reward, how shall we escape if we neglect so great a salvation, which at the first began to be spoken by the Lord, and was confirmed unto us, by those who heard him?[296]

The point here is that we cannot escape. Faced with the rejection of what can lead us to Christ, we replace him with something less suitable in acceptance that condones our chosen sin of disobedience. Disobedience defames the validity of scripture, and it cheapens the scripture's authority and that of Christ. Disobedience belittles faith to the point of raising us through works toward being God's equal, and this becomes acceptable in life.

The Sin of Unthankfulness

The issue with unthankfulness is intended blessing. Unthankfulness has the air of expectant entitlement. The sinful nature of humans looks at the blessing and cursing of God not as a demanded expectation imposed upon them but as an indication that they deserve something different. People do not desire to be judged for their choices of behavior and expect entitlement of blessings. They exhibit ingratitude for the help given them and refuse to even say thank you. Christ said, "Love your enemies, and do good, and lend, hoping for nothing in return. Your reward shall be great, and you shall be the sons of the Highest. For He is kind to the unthankful and to the evil."[297] The sin of unthankfulness treats people and God like they are their own personal slaves in life.

The term *thankfulness* suggests the giving of worship. The practice of thankfulness shows reverence toward God and does not bemoan the condition of life or demand for better. Our worship is the powerful praise that is dispensed in the direction of an object deserving of that praise. Thankfulness does not throw us a curve when conditions in life are tainted by disbelief or by putting our pleasures aside. In repentance, what remains for worship is appropriateness. Thankfulness is the state of grace expressing gratitude for the trials in our lives, testing our faith, and then giving God our worship. Even in our trials, persecutions, and grievances we have against our faith, we experience the favor of God that requires our gratitude. It is graciousness toward God for testing our faith; in so doing, we gratify his love for us. We glean happiness in this well of gratitude of God's graciousness.

Thankfulness suggests that God is good. In giving thanks to God, David states, "Oh, give thanks to the Lord, for He is good! For His mercy endures forever."[298] However, some are ungrateful to God for his goodness. "Although they knew God, they did not glorify him as God, nor were thankful, but became futile in their thoughts, and their foolish hearts were darkened."[299] Gratitude comes down to the level of behavior: "Whatever you do in word and deed, do all in the name of the Lord Jesus, giving thanks to God, the Father through him."[300] It is in the mix of everyday life; "therefore, by him let us continually offer the sacrifice of praise to God, that is, the fruit of our lips, giving thanks to His name."[301] The gift of praise for the graciousness of God offered to us continually endures forever.

Thankfulness is to be an everyday activity. The activity of gratitude provides us the ability to "give thanks at the remembrance of His [God's] holy name."[302, 303] We are to Serve the Lord with gladness. … Know that the Lord, He is God; it is He, who has made us, and not we ourselves; we are his people and the sheep of his pasture. Enter into His gates with thanksgiving, and into His courts with praise. Be thankful to him, and bless his name. For the Lord is good; His mercy is everlasting, and His truth endures to all generations.[304]

The choice of thankfulness shows gratitude toward God for being God. Within this intimacy of our relationship with him, the gratitude is formed, developed, and nourished. We are to be the same with one another, as Paul wrote to the Colossians, "Above all these things, put on love, which is the bond of perfection. Let the peace of God rule in your hearts, to which, also, you were called in one body; and be thankful."[305] Peace comes from righteousness, and this brings safety to our homes and dwellings.[306] The results of gratitude and thankfulness stem from the one who reigns, and our need is to say, "We give you thanks, O Lord God Almighty, the One who is and who was and who is to come, because you have taken your great power and reigned."[307] However, all changes occur at the level of behavior, and Daniel is our example for gratitude and prayer. Daniel wrote of his experience, "Daniel … went home … in his upper room … knelt down on his knees three times a day, and prayed and gave thanks before his God, as was his custom since early days."[308] The peace from righteousness born from the perfection of love gives thanks to the one who reigns as God, ruling over our hearts, which brim over with the gratitude of praise.

The Sin of Unholiness

> **How much worse punishment, do you suppose, will he be thought worthy of punishment, the one who has trampled the Son of God, and who has counted the blood of the covenant with which he sanctified an unholy thing, and has insulted the Spirit of grace.[309]**

Unholiness is not in the eye of the beholder. Like beauty, the idea that the unholy is acceptable, bound in the image of the beholder, displays the morality of those who hold to it. The idea of having something sacred or sanctified is a strange thing to talk about in a world that holds nothing sacred or sanctified. The world attempts to violate all morality, which does not hold people unaccountable and refuses to succumb to the authority of God. This condoning of a lack of morality, the depreciation of moral character, and the demand of physical participation discredits the authority of God's control over morality. People have an underlying understanding of the difference between right and wrong and elect to disregard it. However, unholy behavior leaves us exposed and profane in our work, while disgracing us through our own behaviors. Moses understood there is an inherent natural understanding concerning what is holy and unholy, or unclean and clean, when he wrote concerning the congregation and upholding what is right: "Throughout your generations that you may distinction between the holy and unholy, between the unclean and the clean."[310] Although Moses knew there were things corrupting humankind, he also knew there is really no need to clarify right or wrong for people, even for the people in the house of God. This knowledge written on the hearts of humanity by God gives us the understanding of what is right and wrong.

We bear the wounds of unholiness. We attempt to justify ourselves so that we are right. We attempt to prove our piousness as human beings with all the purity of God while in this sacredness of a world of woe. Moses knew the folly of wickedness when we wrote, "You shall not do according to all that we do here today, each doing whatever is right in his own eyes."[311] Doing what is right in our own eyes has been the bane of humankind's existence since the adoption of Satan's manifesto with Eve. The justification of our behavior continues long after the time of the law given to Moses, well into the times of the judges, and into present-day life. The example of this is with the sons of Benjamin, while "everyone did what was right in his own eyes."[312] Job's sin was justifying himself instead of God. The scripture reads, "These three men ceased from answering Job, because he was righteous in his own eyes."[313] Solomon, attempting to gather his thoughts for us, wrote, "Do not be wise in your own eyes; fear Jehovah and depart from evil."[314] Bearing our wounds of wickedness alone, God gives us instructions on what to do when confronted with the urge to justify our actions to God or others.

There is nothing like taking responsibility for our own actions. Taking responsibility relieves us from the inherent guilt and shame of the violations of our lives. This allows God's intercession of mercy and grace to be upon us through repentance. God knows our propensity for idolatry, and Solomon knew our need to take accountability for our actions. There is surety for every person willing to see themselves for what they are as God knows them. We come to understand as we read, "All the ways of man are clean in his own eyes, but Jehovah weighs the spirits"[315] and "ponders the hearts."[316] During Isaiah's time, he wrote, "Woe to those wise in their own eyes, and bright in their own sight."[317] We are always justifying our behavior through our own eyes, with a lengthy list of reasons, only to end in the woes of a self-imposed, crushing crisis from which God's punishment of sin comes upon us.

We know that the law is good if a man uses it lawfully, knowing this, that the law is not made for a righteous one, but for the lawless and disobedient, for the ungodly and for the sinner, for unholy and profane, for murderers of fathers and murderers of mothers, for manslayers, for fornicators, for homosexuals, for slave-traders, for liars, for perjurers, and anything else that is contrary to sound doctrine.[318]

We do not have sound doctrine in ourselves unless we have input into our lives from an outside source, like the stability of the Bible. Without the sanctification by hearing the word that changes our hearts, minds, and souls, the morality aligned with God is impossible. It is this alignment with God's standards that ultimately changes our behavior and then our thinking. The law of corruption is brought upon us by Satan's manifesto and the deception of our behavior, our minds, and our hearts becoming contrary to God's laws of holiness.

The Sin of Unnatural Affection

Unnatural affection is a hardening of one's heart. Many times, it is the blatant disposing of common ingredients of healthy relationships. Our first consideration is Paul's discussion of humans' sinful nature, writing that they were "vain in their imaginations"[319] and describing them as having darkened, foolish hearts. These foolish people professed their wisdom as they changed the incorruptible God into the likeness of man.[320] This is a means of making God in their own image and then worshiping their own design of God, a truly unnatural affection.

Thus, we write God out of the picture. It is God who is in control of our lives, yet we issue the commands intended for our own design-qualifying behavior. In addition, the unnatural affairs of lust are dishonorable and dysfunctional sexual acts that exploit us. We see the "changing [of] the truth of God into a lie."[321] This is in our thinking; we oversee our own lives by the standards we set for them. God knew his creation had this condition when he called humanity wicked with their imagination, corrupting the thoughts of their hearts and tarnishing them with evil.[322] Ezra called people with unnatural affection impudent children who were stiff-hearted, making their faces stiff.[323] The unnatural affection can be as simple as self-love, making themselves as God's equal. This worshipping of the self and the pleasure found in the exaltation that idolatry brings results in the vaulting of oneself.

Furthermore, homosexuality is an unnatural affection. The dishonorable sexual exploits described by Paul included activities of homosexuality.[324] Paul understood this condition through the rejection of Christ and the stemming unrighteousness when he qualified the condition, saying,

Therefore God, also gave them up to uncleanness, in the lust of their hearts, to dishonor their bodies among themselves, who exchange the truth of God for the lie, and worship and serve the creature rather than the creator, who is blessed forever, Amen.[325]

According to God's law, "You shall not lie with a male as with a woman. It is an abomination."[326] This abominable thing is a disgusting abhorrence of idolatry, loathed and detested by God. This type of idolatry is formed by unnatural affection for someone of the same sex.

A good example of this hard-hearted condition is an unnatural love for something that is promoted to the position of God. When Moses went to confront Pharaoh concerning the children of Israel, Pharaoh strengthened his stance to keep his slaves under his control. He seized his authority over God, thinking he was stronger than the God of Moses. Pharaoh acted courageously in his strength to overpower God; he fortified his position with binding restraints placed upon his conquered Israeli slaves. At some point God will allow the personal hardening of your heart to go unchecked and unconfronted, and then he will end up hardening it for you, just like Pharaoh.[327] This happens to unbelievers during their continued acceptance of behavior bound in unbelief and unrighteous, which directs unholy and rejected activities.

This burdensome condition of unnatural sin dulls the senses. In this hard-hearted condition, the ability to reason is overly weighty, and every given situation has a troublesome aspect of reasoning. This result of unnatural affection is a crushing, self-imposed crisis, credited to our own structured designs for living. Pharaoh hardened his heart enough to bring God in to do the final hardening.[328] The hardness of Pharaoh's heart resulted from his not listening to God's requirements requested by Moses and then from God punishing his rebellion and insubordination. This type of condition is very heavy and severely foolhardy. It makes life difficult beyond what is necessary and brings judgment by God in its wake.

We see this unrelenting nature of unnatural affection within an overzealous proselyte. In comparison, Pharaoh "sinned still more and hardened his heart, he, and his servants."[329] Then there is the writing concerning the scribes and Pharisees of Jesus day, saying, "Woe to you, scribes and Pharisees, hypocrites.... Make one proselyte, and when ... made, you make him twofold more the child of hell than yourselves."[330] Most people do not see the blind activity of a proselyte as one of unnatural affection and behavior. However, this shows how the impact of the hardness of a man's heart in unnatural affection affects and draws others around them into the dysfunctional activities.

The issue with Moses concerns the heart of unnatural affection. Moses wrote, "Therefore, circumcise the foreskin of your heart, and be no longer stiff-necked,"[331] making the issue of unnatural affection a condition of the heart. It is at this point that we need to pay attention to ourselves in our relationship with God. Moses continued, writing, "Take heed to yourselves that your heart may not be deceived, and you turn aside and serve other gods, and worship them."[332] The worshiping of other gods is the byproduct of a hard-hearted rejection; this idolatry of unnatural affection is disdained from the worship of the living God.

The scripture brings with it an understanding of God's provisional plan of salvation. Along with our allegiance to this great God of our salvation comes peace from righteousness, security from integrity, and intercession by a God mediating for us. In the status of this position of unnatural affection within the world, there comes a depreciation of the scriptures, depreciation of our need for God, and a depreciation of the qualification of Christ. The world then requires the deletion of the scripture and its replacement with ideas that are more suitable to up-to-date desires of the choices in what is worshipped. This unrelenting unnatural affection detours us from Christ; this idolatry derailment tends to soothe the desires of our souls. Struck with madness and blindness, our hearts are astonished at the condition of this replacement of God's salvation plan when it comes to our attention.

Part of God's judgment requires our repentance. Repentance helps to get us get back into God's good graces and restores our relationship with him on his terms. Although we do not always do this, waiting to repent can worsen the consequences of impending judgment. We have been warned concerning our condition when we lack repentance. God says, "If you turn your heart so that you will not hear, but shall be drawn away and worship other gods and serve them,"[333] judgement comes. This ultimately puts us under God's judgment process.

We are unable to reconcile our lives to God. Therefore, "Jehovah, your God will circumcise your heart and the heart of your seed, to love Jehovah your God with all your heart and with all your soul, so that you may live."[334] We have an ongoing integration of God's will written on our hearts through the struggle of trials and due to the reeducation of our relationship with God. The final judgment upon our unnatural affection has a solution: "The word of God is living and powerful and sharper than any two-edged sword, piercing even to the dividing apart of the soul and spirit, and of the joints and marrow, and is a discerner of the thoughts and intents of the heart."[335] This word of God presents a lifestyle associated with the living God of creation, provides salvation for all who want it, and lifts Jesus to a point of honor. Faced with our inability to reconcile ourselves to God due to our unnatural affections of worship, God has a job to do. This job requires our lives to become aligned with his through repentance defined by the qualifications we find within our relationship with him in scripture.

The Sin of Unyielding

The result of a hardened heart is the behavior of unyielding. These unyielding behaviors make us unable to build a truce between us and God. This causes our lives to be in suppression against God. God is against pride, which stems from an unyielded heart. God's spirit of grace and mercy cannot be poured out upon us under these conditions. The state of being unyielded makes us inflexible in our faith and in our doctrine concerning the scripture, and it creates a wicked heart against Christ. The scripture does not penetrate our unyielding hearts but keeps pressure on our lives with judgment and correction. Once the alteration of our hearts turns to hardness, this hardness is not apt to give way under the pressure of scripture or reason.

Being untouched by scripture, the heart cannot soften. This void of scripture disallows our drawing close to Christ and causes our hearts to remain hard. This condition breeds evil and contempt against Christ. When our lives are not compliant to the scripture, self-justification causes deviations from God's standards. Then these behaviors, these accepted sins, are validated by self-justification. The hardness of our hearts comes from the condition of nonsubmission. The disregard of God's love, grace, and mercy becomes a way of life. This nonpliable condition caused by unrepentant hearts becomes to us as a way of life—a resolute, uncompromising, unbending, and unshakeable way of life—that we justify with our own reasoning.

This justified reasoning comes through our own eyes and in our own design. Those who have this unwavering condition seek to discredit the scripture, disbelieve God's authority, seek to take God's place, establish themselves among the gods, worship the creation, and take on an irretractable position in life against having a relationship with God and with no repentance. This determined stance of obstinate and stubborn behavior calls the scripture a lie and God less than God. Adamant passion from this tenacious condition holds persistently for the purpose of justifying dissolution of God—the replacement of his word in exchange for something less demanding against this sin of unyielding. This becomes a mandatory statement for self-preservation in life but not eternity. Regardless of the facts, reasons, or scripture, people with unyielding hearts are in a contrary position to themselves and to Christ.

The Sin of the False Accusation

The tendency to blame others comes from an unnatural state of self-importance. So many times, an unyielding condition stems from having a hard heart with unnatural affection. This actively lives in our hearts, accusing God of lies. The inability to take responsibility for our actions and beliefs falsely justifies our positions. Even when it is contrary to the scripture, falsely justifying our positions is the nature of the impossible state of humankind's sinfulness. We record an encompassing protest to Christ's position. The sin is in raising lesser beings and things to a position that is better than his. This sin of false accusations is the bearing of untrue things.

We cheat Christ out of his true position as the son of God. The commandment from God is "you shall not bear false witness against your neighbor."[336] Yet this bearing of things that are untrue is the shame of a witness's testimony against Jesus, the Prince of Peace. We swindle Christ out of his authority and disregard his true position as the son of God. This duplicates Satan's manifesto in our own lives, making us act as if we are God's equal in quality, position, authority, and ability. We qualify things not scriptural as true and then accept them without reservation, disqualifying Christ and his atonement with all the requirements of God for sin and repentance.

We make false accusations in an attempt to meet God on our

own terms in the presence of others. Today's world pressures us to undo God's authority. The ineffective presence of God exchanged for hedonism becomes people's chosen passages for prestige and status. It becomes their own authority of their making. Moses wrote, "You shall not raise a false report. Do not put your hand with the wicked to be an unrighteous witness."[337] However, when people misrepresent the scripture, change its writing for their own prestige of authority, and replace God for their own significance, this is a false report causing evil ruin. This is a desolating destructiveness for the relationship with Christ, keeping us in our sins. False witnessing becomes a useless guile. It is a rushing tempest of exchanges from the foundation of scripture concerning Christ for anything to bolster our chosen sins.

Once again, we face the issue of deceit. This comes from a false witness: "He, who breathes truth shows forth righteousness, but a false witness deceit."[338] Deceit requires judgment resulting from this false witnessing. "If a false witness rises up against any man to testify a falling away against him, then both the men, who are disagreeing shall stand before Jehovah, before the priest, and the judges, which shall be in those days."[339] This scripture calls for two people to face judgment. The unrighteousness of false accusations is a violent exchange intended to gain control over others. It is a dominating manipulation of words and truth, which mistreats the information of God in cheapening ways and deceitful false statements.

The Sin of a Lack of Self-Control

> **These, as unreasoning natural brute animals having been born for capture and corruption, speak evil of things that they do not understand. They will utterly perish in their own corruption, being about to receive the wages of unrighteousness, deeming indulgence as pleasure in the daytime, and reveling in the spots and blemishes, feasting along with you in their deceits, having eyes full of adultery and ever ceasing from sin, alluring unstable souls, having**

> **a heart exercised with covetousness. They are cursed children who have forsaken the right way and have gone astray, following the way of Balaam the son of Beor, who love the wages of unrighteousness, but had reproof of his lawbreaking, a dumb ass speaking in a man's voice, held back the madness of the prophet.**[340]

The lack of self-control is a sin of indulgence. At the core of a lack of self-control is an obsession, an addictive behavior. In the quote above, we see the nature of a lack of self-control in the example of the corruption of behavior. Although we consider adultery to be sex outside of marriage, adultery is considered idolatry, a scriptural and an overt act of a lack of self-control. This comes in a form of covetousness adapted as an acceptable form of right living. The scripture defines this lack of being pure and holy before God as unacceptable. When we engage in hard-hearted activities that depreciate God's word and replace it with something else, our spiritual sensitivity dies. This spiritual desensitization leads to the promotion of a lack of self-control, which is untenable and becomes a dominant position of indulgence.

The validation of the vigor of passion requires an authority. This authority must come from an anointing and the exercise of the scripture's power. Without a guidepost to align our lives, we are overtaken by a lack of continence, moderation, and abstinence. Stemming from a foundation that lacks God's presence and the impact of the scripture to align righteous behavior, we replace those with false premises and then base our lives on them. These unfounded false premises have arguments that mix both true and false statements—an eclectic incontinence of faith. One of the fruits of the Spirit of God is self-control.[341] When integrating God's standards into our lives, we must behave in ways that align with the scripture. There is no law governing our betterment resulting from God's influence. We become powerless through our lack of self-control, which is against our relationship with Christ. Our denial of Christ and of the need for repentance stems from our not accepting what the scripture suggests and leads us to a lack of self-control.

We can engage in a healthy process of change toward self-control. It begins with discipleship that is based on our relationship with Christ and then exhibited in our lives so that it is passed on to others. This process starts with diligence that requires a foundation of scripture, and our knowledge of scripture produces a trust in Christ and the Father of heaven. With consistent interaction with God, our Father, and Christ through consistent prayer and study of the scripture, we develop faith. Over time, this faith gains experiential knowledge of God's ways, his dealings, and how Christ deals with us. This is when self-control develops.

Self-control becomes an everyday occurrence for those with circumcised hearts. Our behavior begins to align with God's commands, and repentance becomes normal. Gleaning an understanding of the processes of God and how he works in our lives, we begin to learn the art of waiting, the virtue of patience. This patience allows us to stop participating in sinful behavior with the help of the Spirit of God. We do not react to our trials with an overt responsiveness but with a responsiveness that produces an endurance in life. Thus, the godliness in our lives comes through our adoption of a way of life with Christ, and because of our faith in him, we live it. During this development of discipleship, we begin to have love for our brothers, sisters, and neighbors.[342] Therefore, through Peter's understanding, we develop maturing fearlessness in our lives, and this diligence leads to the pinnacle of brotherly love. Gleaning at the stage of self-control becomes the fulcrum of our Christian lives.

Not having self-control is a hindrance. We enclose ourselves in a jail of our own making when we lack it. We are blinded and deafened by the darkness of our minds. Our acceptance of something other than Christ and the foundation of scripture blinds us to our condition. We carve a retrogressive groove within ourselves, leaving God at the edge of our untouched lives. Wondering why we do not have a right relationship with God yet, we continue moving farther away from him daily. This makes our hindered lives hollow and without value as we question why God is against us.

A lack of self-control has a necessary process of self-justification. We do not spare ourselves in this process of self-justification, for we are unmerciful judges. While we are our own worst critics, our blindness to the scripture and our damaged relationships with Christ disqualify us as good judges in our own lives. While engaging in a life that lacks self-control, with wrong action and a displaced faith, we justify our blindness. Without an understanding of scripture, we assemble lives through self-indulgence, and this becomes acceptable and condoned. This unrepentant behavior condemns us and pits us against Christ. We assemble people with similar beliefs and knowledge to reinforce our positions. We rule over ourselves with a rod of unmerciful iron, not with faith in Christ. When we refuse to observe the law of God through scripture, and find ourselves under his judgment because of it, we refuse to understand the freedom of God's gift of salvation through Christ. We need to accept our condition through repentance. The imprudence of a lack of self-control become a reproach resulting from self-justification.

The Sin of Savageness

The term for "savage" in the Old Testament and the New Testament is the same. The only mention of savagery in the New Testament is in 2 Timothy. The nature of this sin makes us disregard morality, which causes our lives to descend into savagery. Upon the removal of a scriptural foundation that controls our morality, we are at the mercy of both the designs imposed upon us in life and our own intentions of godhood demands. It is a savage process ordering the exchange of scriptural morality for hedonistic behavior.

This savage corruption from sin is a decaying ruin built into our lives. The nature of savageness exemplified for us is the insight concerning Simeon and Levi, as written, "Let their anger be cursed, for it was fierce; and their wrath, for it was cruel,"[343] showing their savagery. Filled with anger and rage, morality is averted, and we engage in unrighteous and unholy behavior that ruins our lives and many times the lives of others. It is a savage process that orders the exchange of scriptural morality for anything else.

Some would say God is savage. When the earth was filled with violence during the time of Noah, God killed every living thing on the planet. He did this because the whole earth was corrupt before him.[344] Stemming from a lack of repentance and of the cleansing infusion from God's grace, people chose to be isolated in their own savagery and rejected God. The removal of all was the result of this choice. Practicing violence in action, thought, and speech makes us wrong, and living a savage life is an unjust gain of peace by domination, manipulation, and control. Lacking scriptural knowledge leaves us to our own defined savagery.

We never consider the removal of scripture as a violent act, yet in every case, the studying of scripture brings morality and changes of heart concerning Christ. The act of removing from God's people the scripture that leads to Christ is one of savagery. Within this stagnant arena of hypocrisy, religion leads us toward the violence of hedonism, self-effigy, and self-justification. When sin reigns, the required sentence of judgment comes upon us. In the aftermath of judgment, the mandatory consequence for our behavior is a savagely violent act.

Savagery comes from the gain gleaned from the wrongs of sin. Unrighteousness strips from us the relationship with Christ and the Father of heaven. In addition, we are subject to maltreatment when the stripping of scripture occurs. The void fills with an increasing necrotic pus of contempt for God and depreciates the concept and value of Christ. Even people of God can have cruelty in their hearts, not unlike Simeon and Levi, who literally had stabbing weapons noted as "instruments of cruelty"[345] at their disposal. However, cruelty is not just another aspect of violence, like guns, knives, or nuclear weaponry. It can include our behavior toward God and the use of our tongues regarding others.

There are other means of savagery, such as subtle hostility, contemptuous superiority, and more. There is the weapon stemming from doubt that creates deception. The violence of cruelty can come simply from the furnace of our souls, with the pot of resentment and pain that uses our tongues as the weapon of violence. All of these create hostility to scripture, and with that hostility leading away from a relationship with Christ, the result is a violent life of rebellion toward God.

The violence of sinful acts covertly pillages people's life foundations. Violence makes a putrid sore of the soul, especially when issues from the mouths of the wicked. The psalmist wrote, "Swallow up, O Jehovah, and divide their tongues,"[346] which referred to the issues of violence, division, lack of harmony, and fighting. Violence can come from the disagreements concerning the validity of the scripture, a doctrine, the relationships with Christ, who God is, and the nature of what Christ has done for us. In Psalms 72:14, the psalmist wrote, "He shall redeem their soul from deceit and violence; and their blood shall be precious in his sight."[347] Violence encompasses the severing bisection of oppression, cutting away parts of our souls. Violence becomes a source of treachery, eating away at the foundations of our souls.

The whole issue of violence is about God in our lives. Violence depreciates God and the scripture, making them null and void. This condition leads us to a point of mockery, as we become reproachable.[348] The scripture becomes a disgrace, exposing us and stripping away our dignity by defamation. The evidence of our need for salvation, faith in Christ, and lighting of our paths becomes blatant. Violence ruins our concept of scripture, the sovereignty of God, and the value of Christ. It ravages our peace with great swelling insolence. This savagery devastates our faith, with the only term given to it being violence against Christ.

The result of savagery is an unjust gain. Savagery plunders our souls through our breaking and preying upon others. While covetousness fills us with want for something that is not ours to have or be given, savagery schemes to get it. Many times, as is written about churchy people, the "prophets are proud, men of deceit; her priest have defiled the sanctuary; they have done violence to the law."[349] When we are under the law of works, the removal of the word from our lives leaves a destructive violence swelling up in strife and contention with God.[350] The exertion of idolatry replacing the scripture is an overwhelming advantage of the wickedness facing us and our working relationships with God, Christ, and others.

Many times, savagery is an undefendable position. The grievance of savagery judges us by our behavior. Savagery shod with the contesting of and grappling with any lack of scripture's validity causes a wrangling of faith in its controversy. This dismounted toil away from God's salvation by faith through hearing of the word leaves only contempt. As a frothing bubble of unimportance fills treachery against God, thus history repeats itself. Unjust gain of authority comes to wound, dissolve, and break our relationship with Christ through the removal of the impact gleaned from scriptural referencing. This action makes us sick, weak in faith, and grieved in spirit. When entreating the condition of savagery, we succumb to something other than the design of God for us. Whirled into a perverted version of faith, misrepresentations of the relationship with Christ result. This savagery changes us into self-proclaimed orators against the scripture, Christ, and ultimately God.

The Sin of Despising Good

> **We know that all things work together for good to those who love God, to those called according to his purpose.[351]**

Today's world accepts that all is good. Although this is a misquote of Paul's letter to the Romans, the deception is one of sin being acceptable and condoned as good. Some people would suggest that despising what is good is an all-out assault on the Christian faith. The problem with despising what is good is that worship can be of the church itself in prejudicial superiority. It argues that sinful practices and hedonism are acceptable and honorable in life. The removal of biblical letters sets in motion the act of despising what is good through a lack of confrontation of behavior, faith, and worship. This, simply put, is a rejection of Christ. Despising what is good replaces the worship of Christ with anything in his creation. The undermining of faith in exchange for something less intimate than a relationship with Christ results in the worship of anything.

One example of an accepted sinful practice is necromancy, or seeking advice from the dead. Necromancy is a despised sin according to scripture, a form of demonic idolatry. In fact, it is a form of demonic spiritual guidance. It manifests in talking to the dead and is considered demonic possession in some circles. Removing the foundation of scripture and exchanging the truth for an alternative becomes demonic in nature. The virtuous dynamic of intimate relationship integrity with God becomes a thing of the past, and Christ becomes a distant memory. Satan then becomes the leader of the demonic infusion.

Once again, to reiterate, consideration of Satan's manifesto of being God's equal is a good thing in the world. This disappointment was delegated to humans, whom God created, because they adopted this as a better alternative to his paradise. The dishonesty of this exchange despises the validity of God, as humans attempt to become God's equal. Being God's equal—that is, an ascension of a human being to the position of God's authority—is humans' dream adapted from Satan's manifesto.

The hostility toward the concepts contained in the Bible comes with unreasonable suggestions as alternatives. The Bible then is normally considered unreliable and is suggested to discredit itself when discussed. Although the Bible has been the most documented set of written texts in the world and has the highest amount of archeological evidence proving its history, it is discounted. Yes, the Bible is considered unbelievable despite all of its provable facts. Those coming against it make a savage exchange of hostility for the virtues of salvation through faith. In the place of scripture is a promotion of a self-affirming godhood, which is taught in the world as acceptable. This becomes a self-defining validation concerning accountability and responsibility for an ascended godhood. This promotional loss of virtue that is born of the Bible ends in a land of perfection. This perfection is filled with undefined goals and unachievable objectives, and it is hostile in the requirements assumed by humans.

Sin leaves its mark on humankind. We can never attain perfection. The fondness found in the church is associated with perfection for perfection magnifies itself amid and identifies itself above others while qualifying the credentials of God as less than they are. Thus, we have a myriad of denominations attempting to boast that one is better than another, promoting a specific issue over the rest as being the point of doctrine needing adherence. This beauty in the virtue of salvation is lost in the morass of prideful prejudice with the intimate loss of the relationship with Christ. The God of salvation escapes the view of those involved. The experience of the good coming from the grace of God is lost with the mark of sin left upon us.

The Sin of Being a Traitor

Many people would never accept the idea that they are traitors to God. People say, "I do not believe in God," or "I am not a part of religion." Yet they accept the creation as something to worship over the creator. Being a traitor to the God of creation is an apparently common condition.

However, being a traitor to God is not just idolatry. Surrendering our worship for Christ to some aspect of the creation is an attempt to subjugate God to us. Giving away the worship or praise that is due God is flaunting defection from our creator. We exchange the scripture for some other pattern of discipleship that is ongoing. We develop standards that are not God's, making us deserters of God as well as gods in our own eyes. The psalmist knew this when he wrote, "I saw the traitors and was grieved, because they did not keep your word."[352] It is traitorous to cover up God's authority with our own, which is a covert act of pillaging God's authority.

Many people consider their uncontested behavior as acceptable.

Treasonous behavior starts with the invalidation of the scripture in exchange for standards that are not our own. Pillaging from treasonous behavior leaves us naked and unable to define what God requires for us. This creates doubt and uncertainty of salvation and the need to work our way into God's good graces. Solomon wrote, "The integrity of the upright shall guide them, but the crookedness of traitors shall destroy them."[353] Their deception as traitors is acceptable, their morals are acceptable, their teachings are acceptable, and their lack of honor toward the scripture that proves Christ is also acceptable. This becomes their norm. Losing interaction with the scripture results in being a traitor, which means not honoring God. This is the quality of humans' deception as a replacement.

The redefining of Christ is a traitorous act. The redefining of scripture changes the character of Christ, and redefining morality is treason against God. Doing so adopts the Satanic manifesto in attempting to usurp God's position and authority over our lives. We become active participants in the satanic rebellion against God. This distortion of the scriptures exchanges the truth for a deception and a lie. It is a vicious subversion of the integrity of faith in the relationship with Christ. In addition, teaching the scripture becomes illegal, immoral, irresponsible, and heretical, and faith in Christ becomes treasonous against the world. We become what the Bible suggests—wretched[354] in the wake. We do not stand against it but accept the fallacy replacing Christ. As the scripture of faith wrenched from us becomes a normal life requirement, Christ's dominance in our lives lowers.

Nothing is stable in this manipulated blindness of faith. At first this makes no sense to the argument of treason. Solomon went on to write, "Good understanding gives favor, but the way of the traitor is ever flowing."[355] However, the combination of the constant teaching of the worship of creation and the indoctrination of indictments against God, Christ, and scripture have become an ongoing education in people's lives. This is an attempt to exchange a lack of understanding of treason against God for something lesser in nature. This is the exchange brought about by treason, making life harder without the knowledge of God.

The sin of being a traitor to God clears the foundation of faith. The lack of scripture, which is a lack of knowledge of God and of Christ, leaves us in one condition—wretched. As Hosea wrote, "Like Adam, they have broken the covenant. They have acted like traitors against me there."[356] Leaving the scripture behind as ineffective is something other than the knowledge of Christ. Although Hosea focused on Israel, the apple of God's eye, the whole world has taken this mantle and made it their own. The support process gleaned from the Bible to create the foundation and support from God and Christ has lost its influence for feeding intimacy with God.

Removing scripture from our lives is an act of war on Christianity. It shatters the relationship with Christ into pieces of forgetful experiences and creates a foreign country cut from Satan's manifesto. Solomon wrote, "I said in my heart, concerning the matter of sons of men that God might reveal them, and that they might see that they themselves are beast."[357] The winnowing and sifting of the relationship with Christ—born from the foundation of scripture's clarification, examining the requirements of holiness and righteousness, and replacing the Bible and living without it—lowers the threshold for humankind's deception, dishonesty, and contempt for God in treasonous forms of rejection.

The Sin of Being Reckless

Having no foundation of influence through Christ or the scripture creates an atmosphere of recklessness. Without the foundation of God's presence and guidance and left to our own devices with the precipitating consequences, we pay the price for our sin. We become heady, perceiving we are acceptable by the standards provided for us by the traditions of humans. We become a "hired worthless and reckless person, who follow"[358] in blind submission. "Faith comes by hearing and hearing by the word of God,"[359] but as neonates in blind submission to a lack of scriptural foundation, we become reckless. This stems from this uncontested blindness to the scripture. This recklessness in life is vanity of behavior.

We fall headlong into a life with a reckless vanity. Our relationships with Christ are out of balance, flying in moral freefall. Blindness is always in the form of worshipping an idol in life as a replacement for the living God. The content of our foundation becomes empty of power and feels worthless, having a form of godliness and denying its power.[360] The scripture's relevance to the reader who is led astray by Satan's manifesto is the example of this uncontested blindness of reckless vanity.

Faith is not blind submission. It is irresponsible to consider it so. Faith built over time comes from God's foundation of communication[361] through the qualification of scripture, prayer, and sometimes direct answers in experience. The system of faith bred from trust results from this interaction with God in building the knowledge of himself over time. The ways of his consistent intercession over time build reliable assurance, which is trust. Trust resigns itself to faith, knowing God will act a certain way and has all things under his control.

We are not worthless, empty vessels. Poured out for his glory and honor, we are not intended for our own pleasures and purposes. Our desolation of power in creation is ruinous by the destructive reduction of Christ's value. With the world in judgment, we rush to exchange God's word for human traditions. This recklessness and vanity is the evil vileness of idolatry, making Christ useless and common. This is the epitome of recklessness with God.

An example of the vanity through recklessness is Pharaoh. Pharaoh disregards the word of God through Moses to let his people go. The recklessness of Pharaoh in increasing his demand upon the slavery of the children of Israel to work harder was relentless. The vanity of Pharaoh's mentality forces them, saying to "not let them [children of Israel] regard vain words,"[362] associated with their worship of the living God. The people forced to obey in blind submission to the untruth of Pharaoh's authority were with the sham of slavery over them. Later, when the children of Israel were freed into the wilderness, God gave them guiding commandments. Moses recorded God's requirements as, "You shall not take the name of Jehovah, your God in vain. For Jehovah will not hold him guiltless that takes his name in vain."[363] While the world of Pharaoh thought he was the ultimate authority in life, God proved his recklessness and vanity.

This bubble of isolation makes the relationship with God unimportant. Blind submission exchanges part of the creation in frothy recklessness for Christ. Job understood the wickedness of the condition of vanity. He wrote, "He [God] knows vain men; and when he sees wickedness, will he not search it?"[364] God's search of the hearts of wicked men ends only in judgment when the lack of repentance is present. "Surely a man walks about like a shadow,"[365] which is nothing more than a phantom of an illusion in vanity. This attempts to resemble the shade of God's holiness and justified righteousness. The exchange for God becomes the figure of an idol worshipped over God's true value. This develops an oppression for idolatry due to our unfit relationship with God in our lives.

The result of our recklessness is a lack of stability. This instability comes from the lack of scripture and prayer as guidance in life. In exchange for scripture and prayer, the traditions of humankind can say, "Surely, I have made my heart pure in vain, and washed my hands in innocence."[366] It is reckless not to accept and recognize the workings of God. For surely, "unless Jehovah builds the house, they labor in vain, who builds it; unless Jehovah keeps the city, the watchman stays awake in vain."[367] This is the very reckless work in our relationship with God. That is not having him in your life to build it. It is written of God, "I have not spoken in secret, in a dark place of the earth. I did not say to the seed of Jacob, seek me in vain. I, Jehovah, speak righteousness, I declare things that are right."[368] It would be reckless without the guidance and understanding of a God who declares things that are right. Jesus, the Son of God, said, "In vain they worship me, teaching for doctrines the commandments of men."[369] Here, he talks about the recklessness and instability of

Pharisees and others of his time. Whether by doubt, exchange, or robbery of the relationship with God, the removal of the stability of scripture for insight into the relationship with Christ is devastatingly reckless.

We have the same issues with recklessness today. Society takes us away from the foundation of scripture and prayer, the two things that promote the worship of Christ. Everything else makes it vanity. We see this removal of Christ today in schools, government, and even laws concerning therapy and conversion. In many cases, Christianity is considered the next form of terrorism in the world. This concept has become the standard of thought. Paul warned us of this type of reckless blind submission in writing to the Colossians: "Beware lest anyone rob you through philosophy and vain deceit, according to the traditions of men, according to the elements of the world and not according to Christ."[370] To Titus, Paul wrote of the recklessness of what was confronting him at the time, writing, "Avoid foolish questions and genealogies and contentions and strivings about the law, for they are unprofitable and vain."[371] The point is this: we exchange the foundation of scripture for other authorities designed by others. Through the empty falsehood and reckless condition of idolatry, anyone not worshipping God experiences avoidance of the scripture and of a relationship with Christ.

The Sin of Pride

Pride is the foundation for Satan's manifesto imposed upon us. It is a high-minded illusion that consumes us. It inflates us into thinking that we are God's equal or can become his replacement. It puffs us up to the point that we think we can critique God's word, rejecting it in exchange for our own designs and standards. God said, "I will break the pride of your power, and I will make your heavens like iron and your earth like bronze."[372] It is hard for anyone to accept that they are powerless and God is in charge. Despite our thoughts or feelings about it, pride fills our lives. Arrogance grows along with great, swelling pride. Some exchange God's glory for their own religion of pride. There is a measure of excellency in the swelling pomp of outdoing God and writing him off for our own upgrade to godhood.

Human pride rises in mounting ways. Pride is a fundamental issue of being God's replacement. We learn that, someday, in the lives of others, we can play at being a god. Samuel wrote, "I know your pride and the naughtiness of your heart."[373] And although family members can be the cruelest of people in our lives, we can see the seething arrogance coming from the insolence of pride. Hezekiah was humbled for the pride of his heart,[374] and in our own elation of grandeur, our arrogance of accomplishment soars into haughtiness. We, at times, need humbling by God to put us in our place and lead us to begin our worship of God again. Our disrespect urges us at the most importune time to capture this emboldened state of our actions, position, or status, never giving God his just due. Job referred to pride when writing, "God will not withdraw his anger; the allies of the proud lie prostrate beneath him."[375] Pride is an exaltation of ourselves over God's providence in our lives, thinking we can triumph over God for our own agenda.

Arrogance backs our pride. Pride struts its haughtiness, making us think of ourselves as better than God himself. Obadiah wrote, "The pride of your heart has deceived you,"[376] which aligns with what Jeremiah wrote: "The heart is deceitful above all things, and desperately wicked; who can know it?"[377] The idea of listening to our hearts and not to the scripture is one of the most deceptive suggestions. The heart is looking for a reason to be better than God or Christ and never judged for it. It is "through the pride of his face the wicked will not see him; there is no God in all his schemes,"[378] and this is our state when we write God out of the picture. We write God off as being inadequate, reducing him to a forfeited position. Solomon understood this: "The fear of Jehovah is to hate evil; I hate pride, and arrogance, and the evil way, and the wicked mouth."[379] So many people do not understand that their speech takes away God's glory in exchange for their ascension to the creator's position. The result of pride is we have no God in our schemes. We remove the foundation of scripture and elevate ourselves to the status and position of better than God. This is the price tag for people today who try to be god of their own lives.

The Sin of Loving Pleasure

Paul suggests to Timothy that we are lovers of pleasure rather than lovers of God. The problem with this issue is how to define *pleasure*. Do we define it as something hedonistic or just a satisfaction of having done the right things in life? Is it a stain of a chosen sin in which we indulged or just a development of a new neophyte kept from going astray? The issue with the term *pleasure* is in the measurement of how you define it.

We shall attempt to define *pleasure*. Beth-Eden was a house of pleasure in Syria during the time of the Old Testament, where Baal worship was commonplace. This suggests that the sin of pleasure is associated with sexual preferences. Pleasure is normally associated with the soft and pleasant living activities of a voluptuous life. However, this is not always the case. Pleasure might come with the relief of shame, guilt, or even responsibility, while leveling God to our size. It is pleasurable to not have our behaviors required to measure up to God's standards or to be accountable in judgment with consequences for our behavior. Pleasure can be animalistic, with the vitality of breathing in an obsessive idolatry, adulterating our relationship with God. However, pleasure has a way of refreshing the soul, like a breath of fresh air, when appropriate. Yet when it comes from relinquishing God's authority, depriving us of the credibility of his word, or exchanging God's glory for something in the creation, the pleasure of a sinful obsession becomes idolatry. Thus, the issue with defining *pleasure* is associated with who or what is defining it.

We can be pleased with the new neophyte who has decided to come on board with Christ, laden with desire to be the best witness for Christ. This neophyte feeds on the discipleship training through the study of scripture, prayer, and leadership. Repentance is commonly enmeshed in the life of the neophyte. Many may defect, thinking that excommunication from fellowship is forever. The foundation of scripture is sure, and prayer enlisting God's help directs us to follow the right path. The pleasure is in repenting of the matter and thereby repairing the relationships with Christ and our Father in heaven. God is delighted when we return to stay, which resolves the matter of cost to your soul in repentance.

This is not to say that repentance is a bad thing, nor is it to say that being a neophyte with a new relationship with Christ is a bad thing. The point is having a relationship with God through Christ. This has become undesirable to the masses through the traditions of humankind. God is being unwritten from their hearts by the constituent validity being usurped by their traditions. Although this inclines a person to bend to the will of a religious society, it delights in the neophyte's adherence to the will of the group. This makes us feel good, needed, and well with a blissful glee, becoming part of a clinging love by joining in the deliverance of someone's soul for the good of the religious system. We replace Christ in our lives with an idolatry of alienation from God and put the religious system in his place.

The restraint of a religious system reduces God to a set of rules. It nullifies God with the overt control through the mass constituency and a systematic replacement of some dogma in the religious system. The concept of repentance becomes a dedication to the religious system and not an alignment to God's standards and ways in life. This type of pleasurable satisfaction for the purpose of human connections refrains from researching the scriptures for their moral and spiritual validity. The refusal to honor the scripture's importance in our lives engenders a blind submission. The darkening of faith through blind submission withholds the truth of the scripture, changing it to suit the religious system. This spares no person involved in the system. Blind submission is preserved upon pain of ostracizing, which is alienation from the religious belief system. Likened to the pains of death, this banishing of people born in the religious community creates fear of isolation from God. The impact of this pain from a lack of scriptural context is reduced to rules of acknowledging the religious system as more important than Christ.

Fear of alienation preserves the adherence to the religious system. The relationship with Christ is, although distorted from the scripture, damaged in the exchange for the religious system's beliefs. Malachi understood this pain all too well when he wrote, "Who is even among you, who will shut the doors, and you not kindle fire on my alter in vain! I have no pleasure in you, says Jehovah of Host. I will not be pleased with an offering from you."[380] Although Malachi's statement is about the children of Israel, we see the mention of pleasure and the approval is a common assent of feeling gratified with the religious system, not in alignment with God. Paul writes so well to the Philippians, "It is God, who works in you both to will and to do his good pleasure."[381] For when we are in relationship with Christ, we have a pleasure in life that is restful in the process of the grinding trials we face. Religious satisfaction is intended to allow adherence to the masses and the disregarding of a scriptural foundation for a relationship with Christ as a faith-based interaction.

The Christian life is based on the foundation of scripture. Christ promotes himself as and proves himself to be interactive. This building of trust in him over time is faith that he will accomplish what he has set out to do. Christ, being our mediator, is the author and finisher of our faith, accomplishing an intimacy of relationship between us. The foundation of scripture provides the ongoing evidence of his interaction with us.

The exchange of the religious system is in contempt of the relationship with Christ. Contempt arises when the fondness of pleasure of the religious system overshadows the foundation of scripture. We devise ways to leave the quagmire of our stagnant lives, attempting to align ourselves with Christ by our own power. When we forget to view the scripture and lace the definition of ourselves in the view of our religious systems, our problems remain unresolved. "Now, the just shall live by faith, but if he draws back, my soul shall have no pleasure in him."[382] And we think we are doing our best in a solitary self-appraisal. Habakkuk wrote, "Behold, the soul of him is lifted up, and is not upright; but the just shall live by his faith."[383] The sensual delight of our self-defined righteousness is only a self-absorbed sensual pleasure. We call it religious edification. Peter had a lot to say about the ongoing idolatry of religious systems and the adultery stemming from its practice. He wrote,

But these, as unreasoning natural brute animals having been born for capture and corruption, speak evil of the things they do not understand. They will utterly perish in their own corruption, being about to receive the wagers of unrighteousness, deeming indulgence as pleasure in the daytime, and reveling in spots and blemishes, feasting along with you in their deceits, having eyes full of adultery and never ceasing from sin, alluring unstable souls, having a heart exercised with covetousness. They are cursed children, who have forsaken the right way and have gone astray.[384]

The Sin of Hypocrisy

Hypocrisy is the sin of exchangeable morality—the soiled condition of a person who speaks one way, thinks another way, and then acts in a third way. This is the condition of having double standards for living. This condition of disbelief is deceptive and dishonest. The person feigns the truth, turning publicly for approval, and believes their own lies of maintaining their faith in the process. The private life of the unbeliever is an unrelenting judge. This private life pretends the foundation of scripture is disapproved and exchanges it for something founded within the creation. This upgrades a person's status to the level of equality with God or his replacement. Hypocrisy dissembles the value of scripture, repentance, the Christian conversion, and the Christian way of life, defocusing faith in a God (Jesus) and disregarding Jesus as the author and finisher of our faith. This is the true nature of hypocrisy.

Hypocrisy causes us to play a part not designed for us. We act as leaven in the lives of others who live by fermented doctrines. The "hypocrite corrupts his neighbor with his mouth; but through knowledge the just shall be delivered."[385] Without the foundation of scripture, corruption comes by the beguiling of enticing words.[386] We appear to be righteous, and yet, we are soiled in impious arrogance, in moral corruption, and in defilement by pride, exchanging God for an idolized something lesser. However, the double-tongued condition of believing one thing and saying another, calling something else God, is always hypocrisy of deception and dishonesty.

The hypocritical condition tells a story with the same characters. Each storyline is built with similar words. An old Dutch saying goes, "Beware of a person with two faces," while Eleanor Roosevelt stated, "It is not fair to ask of others what you are not willing to do yourself." James wrote, "A double-minded man is unstable in all his ways."[387] It is because these two-spirited people are hypocritical; they vacillate between the truth and the lie. James goes on to write of the solution, "Draw near to God, and he will draw near to you. Cleanse your hands, sinners, and purify your hearts, double-minded ones."[388] There is a form of godliness, and yet denying the power of faith to have it is hypocrisy.

We need to clarify doctrine regarding hypocrisy. We gain education through scripture to learn a way of life comparable to that of the Bereans. Their way was to read the Bible and pray every day. These people "were more noble than those of Thessalonica, in that they received the Word with all readiness of mind and searched the Scriptures daily to see if those things were so."[389] We are required to search the scripture to prove the validity and accuracy of things we hear or encounter. The psalmist wrote, "They speak vanity each one with his neighbor; with flattering lips and a double-heart they speak,"[390] describing the actions of hypocrites. It is when we face the lack of scripture that we speak of ourselves as better than we are. We live double lives to protect our pleasures in life, and this is hypocritical.

Christ, being God, is the final judge on any subject. He stated, "Hypocrite! First cast the beam out of your own eye, and then you shall see clearly to cast the splinter out of your brother's eye."[391] We are to examine ourselves in comparison to the scriptures, aligning ourselves with God and allowing him to be the judge of all.[392] In the end, Christ pronounces woe upon those who are deceivers, as their deception comes from their hypocrisy: "Woe to you, scribes and Pharisees, hypocrites! For you compass sea and the dry land to make one proselyte, and when he is made, you make him twofold more the child of hell than yourselves."[393] The hypocrite has a lot to say and, with much enticement, hedges the deception in good-sounding words. And while the scripture is isolated from being a foundation for us, the hypocrisy removes our ability to retrieve accurate information because of the seduction taking place.

CHAPTER 6

INFUSION OF FAITH AS IMPUTED RIGHTEOUSNESS

Now faith is the substance of things hoped for, the evidence of things not seen.[394]

Faith accounted to a person as righteousness is a constant. There are possibly hundreds of examples of this imputed righteousness in the Bible, but we will be discussing only a few of them. Habakkuk wrote, "The just shall live by faith,"[395] which expresses a firm security of fidelity to God for establishing his trustworthiness to us. We can trust God to do his job, and this builds faith. Our persuasion with the confidence of the credence and conviction is that God will do his work in us, making his word good for us. The writer of Hebrews set forth a standard: "Without faith it is impossible to please him, for he, who comes to God must believe that his is and that He is a rewarder of those, who diligently seek him."[396] Faith is an active understanding that God will do his job. Jesus then becomes the author and finisher of our faith as the chief leader of our salvation. Jesus is a completer of our faith in a consummation of building our faith through seen and unseen activities, building trust in his word to us. The writer of Hebrews again wrote,

Therefore, since, we, also, are surrounded with so great a cloud of witnesses, let us lay aside every weight and sin, which so easily besets us, and let us run with patience the race that is set before us, looking to Jesus the Author and Finisher of our faith, who for the joy that was set before Him endured the cross, despising the shame, and sat down at the right of the throne of God.[397]

The issue of faith is one of expectation. Expectation is understanding that God will do the job the way he has defined it. The list of heroes of faith in Hebrews 11 suggests that God promised things in his interaction with them. They had the faith in living before God until they received the gifts promised. These people had the confidence, which they embraced, and had the persuasion, confessing God was going to give it to them. They were nothing more than pilgrims and strangers in places where the faith was given them with a promise of hope.

God was their anchor who offered the promise. He plainly declared to these people a promise, and he remained faithful to that promise over time. This consistency over time bridges for us the trust in his functioning. God's ongoing intercession bears witness to their developing faith with their behavior of trusting him. Faith then is grasping that God is doing his job and understanding that he will continue to do it. Even when we lack faith, our unfaithfulness is apparent, or our inability to meet God's requirements in life is blatant, God remains faithful to his word to us. Faith is never about us but about what God can do. For he is God and not us. The expectation here is "God is not ashamed to be called … God, for He has prepared a city for them."[398] In this list of Hebrews 11, we see the faith of the righteous:

Who through faith subdued kingdoms, wrought righteousness, obtained promises, stopped the mouths of lions, quenched the violence of fire, escaped the edge of the sword, out of weakness were made strong, became valiant in fight, turned to flight the armies of the strangers.[399]

One story is not in the list. So much more can be expressed about the lives of this righteous listed in Hebrews 11. The extent of their faith told as righteousness accounted to them is well documented. However, our first story is a woman who made living arrangements for Elijah. She was satisfied with her life and expressed her need for nothing. This is when Elijah interceded on her account, and she conceived a son. The son died, and Elijah, having compassion on her, raised her son from the dead. It was at this moment of restoration that she acknowledged Elijah as being a man of God.[400] This one woman was not expecting a promise from God or one of God's people; however, the promise came anyway.

The future holds a resurrection for the dead. This resurrection comes with a living judgment that is still pending. Some people in the past tortured others on account of their faith. This was documented and accounted as righteousness of their faith. Some people in the future will be tortured with no deliverance forthcoming, and yet it has been prophesied that some will be delivered from the hands of their enemies. Many look forward to the accounting in the Lamb's book of life. Others do not look forward to being judged and not being in it. Whether believers in Christ or nonbelievers, we all will at some point have to face the creator of all things and be judged for the good and bad in our lives based on God's terms.

Faith perseveres over the clarity of people's hatred. Christ spoke of the subtle and overt cruel hostilities of those against him. People through the ages, with their harsh mocking and violence, have attempted to eradicate Christianity from the world. Presently, we see the hatred of Christians, as their lives are taken from them for their faith. Their endurance in their faith for Christ led them to face this hostile opposition and death. Although some prophets were sawed in two and others slain with the sword, they set an example for us as we face "so great a cloud of witnesses, let us lay aside of every weight and the sin, which so easily besets us, and let us run with patience the race that is set before us."[401] We could wander the deserts, mountains, dens, and caves, and our lot is to "obtain a good report, for God had provided some better things for us."[402] However, when Christians get together, they revel in the glory of Christ, enduring the bonds of jails, incarcerations, imprisonments, and death for Christ's sake.

The Faith of Abel

> **By faith Abel offered to God a more excellent sacrifice than Cain, by which he obtained witness that he was righteous, God testifying of his gifts. By it he, being dead, yet speaks.[403]**

Abel's offering involved the shedding of blood. This is the first appearance of a lamb sacrifice, an offering of blood to cover the sins of the guilty. This sacrifice respected by God[404] and by the Hebrew writer "obtained witness he [Abel] was righteous."[405] The shedding of the lamb's blood was a representation of Christ's blood being shed for the covering and remission of sin. This was accounted to Adam for righteousness through his faith.[406] Jesus, the mediator of the new covenant, is the God who judges all, including the spirits of just people made perfect. That was better than Abel's sprinkling.[407] Christ testified of his gifts as a more excellent sacrifice than a gift born out of the curse.

The actions of Adam continue in life. Death came by this one man, and salvation came by one man, Jesus Christ.[408] We can hear in Solomon's prayer for the temple, as he says for us, "Then hear in heaven your dwelling-place, and forgive, and do, and give to every man according to all his ways, whose hearts you know. For you, you only know the hearts of all the sons of Adam."[409] We are well known to Christ, the author and finisher of our faith.[410] We do not want to just cover our transgressions with our own souls[411] but want to have Christ be our intercessor forever.[412] In the end, God wants from us a contrite heart and a consistency of love for him. As Hosea wrote, "I desire mercy and not sacrifice, and the knowledge of God more than burnt offerings."[413] However, we do not wish to be traitors to God by remaining in his way as obstacles. Thus, Hosea continued, "But, like Adam, they have broken the covenant. They have acted like traitors against me."[414] Christ understands our position and our needs: "If you abide in me, and my words abide in your, you shall ask what you will, and it shall be done to you."[415] This abiding makes mulch for the growth of our faith in bringing our actions into alignment with him. Adam's actions covered sin through the sacrifice of an animal, like in the temple, but Christ made one offering for the remission of sin on the cross for all, forever, to whoever accepts his gift.

The Faith of Enoch

Enoch is an example to follow. He walked with God,[416] and he was known to please him through faith.[417] Enoch was taken from this world because God translated him. Some suggest that Enoch's translation possibly reserved him for another purpose, like for the fulfillment as the olive branch or the candlestick of Revelation.[418] Enoch's story is ongoing because he is still alive for a purpose. There was a counterfeit version of Enoch, through Cain, who built a city to his son Enoch. This was in fact a version of the worship of humankind. It was the prophet Enoch who said, prophesying, "Behold, the Lord come with myriads of his saints to do judgment against all, and to rebuke all the ungodly of them concerning all the ungodly works, which they ungodly did, and concerning all the hard things ungodly sinners spoke against him."[419] a This prophet of God, Enoch, walked with God, had a relationship God, and pleased God through his walk of faith, and God translated him for further work.

The Faith of Noah

> **Noah found grace in the eyes of Jehovah. These are the generations of Noah. Noah was a just man and perfect in his generation. Noah walked with God.[420]**

Noah walked by faith to please God. This grace displayed to Noah was founded on what God deemed in him as the actions of faith. He built the ark was through faith in God. Noah knew God would do all that he said he would do. Noah followed through with it, putting his actions and behavior behind it.[421] Because of Noah's faith and the grace given him, God considered him just and perfect in his wicked generation.[422] "By faith Noah having been warned by God of things not yet seen, moved with fear, prepared an ark to the saving of his house … becoming heir of the righteousness, which is according to faith."[423] Noah was a preacher of righteousness.

The world needed a preacher before the flood's judgment came upon all the ungodly. God did not spare the world or all that was in it,[424] except for Noah and his family. We see that Noah did all that the Lord commanded of him.[425] Noah had this prophesy about him: "This one shall comfort us concerning our work and the toil of our hands, because of the ground, which Jehovah had cursed."[426] Ezekiel wrote concerning Noah and wrote of both Daniel and Job, whose souls found deliverance by their righteousness,[427] but no one else. Christ also spoke of them. This speaks volumes to the dedicated righteousness of these men. It was God, himself, who told Noah to get in the ark because God considered Noah righteous in his eyes.[428] Noah had not been baptized and did not know Christ on the cross. Yet he knew God personally and did what he was instructed. His behavior and belief in what God told him was the faith accounted to him as righteousness. Finally, Peter wrote concerning Christ and Noah,

> Christ, also, once suffered for sins, the just for the unjust that he might bring us to God, indeed being put to death in the flesh, but make alive in the Spirit … when once the long-suffering of God waited in the days of Noah, while the ark was being prepared (in which a few, that is, eight souls were saved through water); which figure now, also, saves us, baptism; not a putting away of the filth of the flesh, but the answer of a good conscious toward God, by the resurrection of Jesus Christ.[429]

The Faith of Abraham

> **Abraham believed God, and it was counted to him for righteousness.[430]**

Another example of faith in Christ is Abraham. God accounted the behavior of Abraham as righteousness. His faith and actions came in the form of active repentance, as he left his old life and followed God's directions by faith. Abraham believed God was good to his word, which was a demonstration of faith. Abraham said that God would provide an offering in place of Abraham's son, saying, "God will provide Himself the lamb for a burnt offering."[431] This prophetic message suggests the offering of Christ in the future and that he will be the lamb slaughtered for the remission of sins. The covenant between Abraham and God was the sign of circumcision, which was the seal of righteousness of faith.

Abraham, by his faith, obeyed God. He was the "father of all those who believe, though they are uncircumcised that righteousness might be imputed to them also."[432] Paul to the Romans wrote of Abraham, "Abraham believed God, and it was counted to him for righteousness, but to him working, the reward is not reckoned according to grace, but according to debt, but to him not working, but believing on Him, justifying the ungodly, his faith is counted for righteousness."[433] Abraham's demonstrated willingness to sacrifice Isaac, knowing God was good to his word about the inheritance offered to him: land for Abraham and his heirs. "He looked for a city, which has foundations, whose builder and maker is God."[434] Like the offering of Christ, Abraham through his faith offered his only-begotten son, concluding "that God was able to raise him up, even from the dead."[435] Abraham's faith was based on his belief that God was good to his word. Abraham's faith in God's word saved him unto the day of redemption.

The Thief on the Cross

The harshest example of faith accounted for righteousness is the thief on the cross next to Christ. He was unable to get down and work his way into God's good graces by righteous living or following God's way and direction, like Enoch, Noah, or Abraham. He was unable at that point to live and come closer to Christ daily through repentance. He could not please him more with an enduring faith like Enoch's translation. He could not stop his own death. He could not get off the cross to go get baptized after his confession of faith. Despite John in Matthew 3, and Peter, stating, "Repent and let every one of you be baptized in the name of Jesus Christ for the remission of sins, and you shall receive the gift of the Holy Spirit,"[436] the thief was unable to do it. Then again, the thief expressed enough faith in his conversation of the heart, as written, "Therefore, repent and convert, so that your sins may be blotted out, when the times of refreshing shall come from the presence of the Lord."[437] He was unable to conduct repentant behavior over time, only saying, "Lord, remember me when You come into your kingdom."[438] Christ spoke to him concerning his faith at that moment: "Truly, I say to you, Today, you shall be with Me in Paradise."[439] Because of this man's simple act of faith by his oral confession and believing in his heart, Christ accepted him and offered him eternal life.[440] Christ accounted his confession to him for righteousness.

CHAPTER 7

INABILITY TO WORK OUR WAY INTO GOD'S GOOD GRACES

Because we cannot work our way into God's good graces, we must meet God on his terms. A holy God cannot accept sin or a sinful life without judgment. The judgment of sin requires death,[441] "for having sinned and come short of the glory of God."[442] "There is none righteous, no not one, there is none that understands, there is none that seek after God,"[443] suggesting no one is capable of really meeting God based on God's standards and specifications for living holy in a righteous, upright life. This means the requirement is to meet God based on his standards, not our inadequacies.

In facing a holy God on his standards, unbelievers must do one of two things. The first is to depreciate Christ's work on the cross, which ends in an empty futility. The other is to accept Christ's intercession of blood on the cross, which changes their lives in accordance with a repentant and circumcised heart. However, as Paul wrote, "I do not set aside the grace of God, for if righteousness is through law, then Christ died without cause."[444] This means we cannot live up to the standards to which we are accountable and that are required by God for holiness. There needs to be another means of restitution other than our own deaths. Thus, we must focus on having faith in Christ: "For Christ is the end of the law for righteousness to everyone who believes."[445] The exchange of the glory of God for something other than what Christ has offered is sin. The exchange of the scripture for something offered by humankind is futility. The futility and sinfulness of exchanges for Christ are evident.

Faith works in us the righteousness of God. So if faith comes by hearing and the hearing by the word of God, then this "Word of God is living and powerful and sharper than any two-edged sword, piercing even to the dividing apart the soul and spirit, and of the joints and marrow, and is a discerner of the thoughts and intents of the heart."[446] We then understand that "all scripture is God-breathed, and is profitable for doctrine, for reproof, for correction, for instruction in righteousness that the man of God may be perfected, thoroughly furnished to every good work."[447] "The wrath of man does not work out the righteousness of God,"[448] as in the process of depriving people of God's word. The deception is in taking the scripture from the believer first and then exchanging it for something made by humans. Thus, faith in Christ provides us the means of the righteousness to be in God's presence.

We begin to see the hypocrisy in the difference between the children of God and the children of the Devil. This is where "everyone not practicing righteousness is not of God, also, he, who does not love his brother."[449] We are to "be found in Him [Christ], not having my own righteousness, which is of the Law, but through the faith of Christ the righteousness of God by faith."[450] This simple believing in Christ through the examination of his word reveals that we "are in Christ Jesus, who of God is made to us wisdom, righteousness, sanctification and redemption, so that, according as it is written, He who glories, let him glory in the Lord."[451] It is the faith in Christ according to what he has done for the remission of sin that overrules and buries the human traditions and the workings of the ungodliness formed from the promotion of Satan's manifesto in our lives.

Our righteousness exchanged for Christ's fulfills our righteous need. If we then "confess the Lord Jesus, and believe in [our] heart that God has raised Him [Jesus] from the dead, [we]shall be saved. For with the heart, one believes unto righteousness, and with the mouth one confesses unto salvation."[452] Paul explains to Titus this issue in detail:

> When the kindness and love of God, our Savior, toward men appeared, not by works of righteousness, which we have done, but according to His mercy, He saved us, through the washing of regeneration and renewal of the Holy Spirit, whom He poured out on us abundantly through Jesus Christ, our Savior, that being justified by His grace, we should become heirs according to the hope of eternal life.[453]

When we face the confrontation of our faith through Christ from the hearing of the word, in the bulk of the scripture, we are faced with the defense of our faith to others. Peter wrote to us,

> If you also, suffer for righteousness' sake, you are blessed. Do not fear their fear, nor be trouble, but sanctify the Lord God in your hearts, and be ready always to give an answer to everyone, who asks you a reason of the hope in you, in meekness and fear; having a good conscience that while they speak against you as evildoers, they may be shamed, those falsely accusing your good behavior in Christ.[454]

CHAPTER 8

A CIRCUMCISED HEART

The issue of faith in Christ comes to a fine point of having a heart circumcised from sin. The idea is a repugnant one for people who are not believers in Christ or are presently involved in a chosen sin. Facing their defense of a chosen sinful behavior fills the air with judgmental statements such as, "Who are you to judge me in my behavior or choice?" and "What gives you the right to judge me?" Although their own behavior condemns them and the reluctance to repent is apparent, this does not release them of the need for a circumcised heart toward Christ. The point of a circumcised heart is to align ourselves with what God has for us to act out in life.[455] A circumcised heart removes the manifesto of Satan from our lives. It stops defining behavior by our own terms. The circumcised heart accepts what the volume of the scripture has to say concerning the love story of Christ. Christ is the atonement for the removal of sin through the shedding of his blood on a cross as the Lamb of God.

A Circumcised Heart

Having a circumcised heart is a command for us. We are to worship God alone, and we are commanded to "therefore, circumcise the foreskin of … [our] heart, and be no longer stiff-necked. For Jehovah, your God, is God of gods, and Lord of lords, a great God, the mighty and a terrible God, who does not respect person nor take a bribe."[456] In our attempt to bribe ourselves by exchanging his word for something else better than God, we assert that our own designs are God breathed—in direct conflict with God's word for us. However, we are under the curse of sin, and God states, "Jehovah, your God, will circumcise your heart and the heart of your seed, to love Jehovah, your God, with all your heart, and with all your soul, so that you may live."[457] We come to understand our limitations and that we cannot do this alone.

God speaks of the consequences of a pending judgment. He says, "Circumcise yourselves to Jehovah, and take away the foreskins of your heart … lest my fury comes forth like fire, and burn, so that none can put it out; because of the evil of your doings."[458] Judgment comes to the uncircumcised heart, and God says, "Let him, who glories glory in this, that he understands and knows Me that I am Jehovah, doing kindness, judgment and righteousness, in the earth, for in these I delight, says Jehovah."[459] We then choose between a circumcised and an uncircumcised heart. As sinful people under the curse of sin, we chose the lesser for our benefit. We desire to have our own lives under our control. A circumcised heart forgoes the pleasure provided by our own design and aligns our behavior, desires, and interactions with God's request of us because it is a better life after all.

CHAPTER 9

THE NATURE OF REPENTANCE

Bring forth therefore fruits worthy of repentance.[460]

The nature of repentance is relief from the effects of sin upon our lives. We can then sigh in relief and breathe deeply, free from the associated fears without a consolation of pity. Repentance is a process of acknowledging our wrong against God and aligning our behavior with his standards of holiness, righteousness, and purity. A life filled with deplorable behavior is nothing more than pitiable. Our conscience may feel uneasy, and yet, it is restorable through repentance. It is the contrition for reformation of our behavior, with this reversal of actions as our chosen and acceptable behavior aligned with his. We might have considered old, sinful behavior as normal. We begin to think differently, hesitating in our actions and reconsidering them. Christ brought to our attention our need to learn mercy and righteousness when Matthew wrote, "But go and learn what this is, I will have mercy and not sacrifice. For I have not come to call the righteousness, but sinners to repentance,[461] and this was echoed by Mark.[462] This an exercise of the mind to comprehend and heed this necessary condition of self-control. The requirement that repentance be mournful is part of the process concerning the expression of our soul regarding past behavior.

We begin to understand the meaning of peace stemming from the remission of sin. Luke wrote, "He said to them, so it is written, and so it behooved Christ to suffer and to rise from the dead the third day, and that repentance and remission of sins should be proclaimed in his name among the nations, beginning at Jerusalem."[463] Sin drives us to grieve our own actions and the consequences of the effects of sin. For it is written, "The Lord is not slow concerning His promise, as come count slowness, but is long-suffering toward us, not purposing that any should perish, but that all should come to repentance."[464] The metamorphosis of our behavior drops our desire to accept, condone, and participate in our old ways of sinful actions.

Repentance is the lack of conformity to the mass constituency. The mass rule for us is not repentance, but as Paul said to the Romans, "Do not be conformed to this world, but be transformed by the renewing of your mind, in order to prove by you what is that good and pleasing and perfect will of God."[465] The conflicts of our conscience are God's design within the human psyche, which leads us to repentance. "For the grief according to God works repentance to salvation, not to be regretted, but the grief of the world works out death."[466] It was John who prophesied Christ's coming as the Lamb of God: "John came baptizing in the wilderness and proclaiming the baptism of repentance for the remission of sins."[467] The final note for the nature of repentance is "this One God has exalted to be a ruler and savior to His right hand to give repentance and remission of sins to Israel, and we are his witnesses of these things. So also, is the Holy Spirit, whom God has given to those, who obey him."[468] However, this extended to all, including the Gentile community:

So that whosoever believes in him should not perish, but have everlasting life. For God so loved the world that he gave his only-begotten son, that whosoever believes in him should not perish, but have everlasting life. For God did not send his son into the world to condemn the world, but so that the world might be saved through him.[469]

CHAPTER 10

THE PROCESS OF REPENTANCE

> **If My people, who are called by My name, shall humble themselves and pray, and seek my face, and turn from their wicked ways, then I will hear from Heaven and will forgive their sin and will heal their land.** [470]

The process of repentance is a simplistically complicated one. The complication comes from our desire in compromising our decision and attempting to lower the standards for our morality, holiness, and purity in repentance. The process of repentance is a simple calling to humble ourselves before God and to walk in his ways. This is not defining of behavior from our own standards. Repentance laced with the corruption of sin does not have the standards of God's mercy for sin. Repentance requires our confession of sin and asking forgiveness while changing our behavior. This process of repentance keeps us in an interactive relationship with God, our Father, and with our Savior, Jesus Christ.

Humble Themselves

Humility is the ability to see yourself through God's eyes. It is very arrogant of people to think less of themselves than what they really are in life and a strange concept of pride to minimize their condition in life as being perfectly OK. Although God talked about the Sabbath's rest, he tells us, "You shall humble your souls."[471] It is when we humble our souls, raising God to his rightful position, that our lives become exalted. Ezra sought God for reasons of his own, through his submission under God's rule and fasting "that we might humble ourselves before our God, in order to seek from him a right way for us and for our little ones, and for all our goods."[472] Repentance is everyone's responsibility toward God. However, so many times, we attempt to define God in our own eyes, under our own terms. Yet "Jehovah, you have heard the desire of the humble; you prepare their heart, you will cause your ear to hear."[473] So God hears the prayer of the humble.

Humility is accepting our place in God's good graces. As written, "For so says the high and lofty One, who inhabits eternity; whose name is Holy; I dwell in the high and holy place, even with the contrite and humble spirit, to revive the spirit of the humble, and to revive the heart of the contrite ones."[474] When sin fills our lives, there is a demand for repentance and the humility of repentance. This position asks for God's forgiveness and requires us to be under God's mercy and judgment of us. "Therefore, whoever shall humble himself like this child, this one is the greater in the kingdom of heaven,"[475] for "He gives more grace. Therefore, he says, God resist the proud, but he gives grace to the humble."[476] Humility is the relinquishing of the satanic manifesto as being God's usurper to be in submission to his authority over us and aligned in our behavior with God's standards of mercy and grace for our lives.

Prayer

> **Let us therefore come boldly to the throne of grace that we may obtain mercy and find grace to help in time of need.[477]**

Prayer is the science of communication with God. In communication, we must define our terms before we can understand each other. The *Easton's Bible Dictionary* says this about the communication of prayer:

It "is converse with God; the intercourse of the soul with God, not in contemplation or mediation, but in direct address to him." Communication with God can take many forms and happen in various ways.[478] In the beginning, "God came walking in the garden in the cool of the day."[479] This was the time of day when Adam had face-to-face communication with the creator of the universe. In this setting, the communication had intimacy and interaction in which God gave Adam his friendship and nurturance.

Meditation is God talking to us. This first takes place for us as we lay the foundation for understanding God by reading the scripture. Paul discussed this value of scripture as he told Timothy it was "profitable for doctrine, for reproof, for correction [and] for instruction in righteousness."[480] Second, the foundation of prayer is the scripture. In addition, our lives have God's handiwork in them, as we listen to the still small voice within us. Although communication from God can come in other ways, we are to have the scripture as the foundation for it. In addition, we are to test the spirit of the communication, and if it does not lead to Christ, then it is wrong.[481] Paul told the Thessalonians to "test everything; hold fast what is good."[482] However, we are the ones communicating with God, and Paul teaches us to test ourselves, requiring this examination of ourselves.[483] In addition, we need to ask ourselves if our activities distract us from the study of the scripture, taking us away from the knowledge of God. Do we need to remove a powerful influence from our lives? The study of the scripture improves your quiet time, leading you in prayer according to God's will, and developing an intimate life with God.

Prayer has a price. When confronted by Eliphaz, Job says, "You shall make your prayer to him, and he shall hear you, and you shall pay your vows."[484] This leaves us with the cost of questioning the price we must pay for our vows. Christ told the church of Laodicea to come buy of him gold purified by fire, white cloths, and salve to anoint their eyes.[485] It is hard to understand our condition and need when we require righteousness in our lives. What keeps us from righteousness are our own compromised lives. We demand to have purity in our lives and yet are corrupted by our condition of being wretched, miserable, poor, blind, and naked. We need the salve of grace to understand the cryptic responsiveness of having the forgiveness from his atonement of grace and mercy. Prayer by repentance changes the consequences of our actions and rewards us by aligning our lives and behavior with God's will in life.

Prayer is for preservation. David sought after God in his prayer, conveying his complaint to him and asking God to "guard his life from fear of the enemy."[486] The scripture leads us to understand what God wants from us, and prayer communicates our needs, our limitations, our reluctance, and our search for God's help. It was Moses who wrote, "Jehovah commanded us to do all these statutes, to fear Jehovah our God, for our good always, so that He might preserve us alive, as it is today."[487] Through the meditation of scripture and prayer, this helps us to remain abiding in Christ.[488] Through prayer, our souls change so that "he [Christ] be enthroned forever before God; appoint steadfast love and faithfulness to watch over [us]."[489] When we observe God's standards and then live righteous lives, we can pray, "Preserve my life, for I am godly; save your servant, who trust in you—you are my God."[490] Having a relationship with Christ and being a part of his family focuses our experience on God, while he makes provision for us and intercedes on our behalf. Our worship then is understanding God, saying to us,

Thus, says the Lord: in a time of favor, I have answered you; in a day of salvation, I have helped you; I will keep you and give you as a covenant to the people, to establish the land, to apportion the desolate heritages, saying to the prisoners, come out, to those who are in darkness, appear. They shall feed along the ways; on all bare heights shall be their pasture; they shall not hunger or thirst, neither scorching wind nor sun shall strike them, for he who has pity on them will lead them, and by springs of water will guide them.[491]

In our prayer lives, God knows what we need before we ask for it.[492] All we must do is use what he has given us to do.

Now is the time for prayer. David understood that the time is now when he wrote, "As for me, my prayer is to you, O Lord. At an acceptable time, O God, in the abundance of your steadfast love answer me in your saving faithfulness."[493] Those standing before the throne and the Lamb of God express a cry, saying, "Salvation belongs to our God, who sits on the throne, and to the Lamb."[494] We cannot fathom the discontent of those who would "neglect such a great salvation."[495] How can we escape without our hearts circumcised from sin, with its remission by the atonement by Christ's shedding of his blood on the cross for us? A broken heart is required for repentance.

We ask God's forgiveness. We say, "You know my reproach, and my shame and my dishonor; my foes are all known to you. Reproaches have broken my heart, so that I am in despair. I looked for pity, but there was none, and for comforters, but I found none."[496] Therefore, we need a quiet time to meet God on his terms. This includes a period for reading scripture and then praying to dedicate our lives, behaviors, and actions to be in alignment with the scripture. "Prayer before the LORD, our God that we might turn from our iniquities and understanding the truth."[497] This is the nature of conversion with our learning from scripture and its application of truth to our lives. During our intimate time with Christ in prayer, we anchor ourselves to the actions in accordance with what we learn in scripture. We then should be "continuing steadfastly in prayer."[498] Faced with asking for forgiveness from God for our sins of the past, present, and future, we are nothing more than clanging brass in the wind of self-repudiation.

This needed prayer is to avoid temptation. We give ourselves "to fasting and prayer … that Satan tempt"[499] us not according to our incontinency. This consistency in studying the word and indulgence of prayer seeking Christ's intercession, help, and provisions for doing his work are the point. We become the witness of Jesus with the "door of utterance, to speak the mystery of Christ."[500] With the door of utterance, we know our place with Christ; know our position with God, our Father; and are faced with our own limitations, our own sins, and our own attempts at taking God's place in life. We avoid temptation of sin and become the witness of Jesus Christ.

We need the prayer of repentance. We need to hear the mercy in life as we lend our ears to be attentive, to hear the prayer confessing sins. We return to God's commandments, redeemed by God's great power and asking that he grant mercy in the sight of humankind.[501] Although James says that the prayer of faith shall save the sick,[502] we know the prayer of faith saves the soul from the soul's sin sickness. This provides us a new nature through Christ to conduct our lives in righteousness, purity, and holiness. It is this confession of our sinful nature, our turning from our sinful ways of usurping God's authority in our lives, that helps us gain forgiveness of sin and heal.

Seek God's Face

Seeking God's face is an act of humility. Many of us have lived our lives to become God's equal. We have sought ways to take God's place or replace his authority in our lives. In our search, we must relinquish our desire to take God's place or being his equal. Moreover, we must understand that "he is a rewarder of those, who diligently seek him."[503] However, instead of seeking our own selfish ways of fulfilling our obsessive need to be superior to others or fill our needs, we are to consider what Christ told us: "Seek first the kingdom of God and His righteousness, and all these things shall be added to you."[504, 505] Christ, our example, can say, "I can of myself do nothing, as I hear, I judge; and my judgment is righteous, because I do not seek my own will, but the will of the Father, who sent me."[506] We need to study the scripture and use prayer to seek God's will. Thus, we need to apply the same standard to our own lives in doing justly, living righteously, and having an intimate relationship with our Father in the same manner as Christ. We can then stand with Zechariah in saying,

The inhabitants of one city shall go to another, saying, let us continue to go and pray before the Lord, and seek the Lord of host. I, myself will go also. Yes, many people and strong nations shall come to seek the Lord of host in Jerusalem, and to pray before the Lord.[507]

When we seek God's face, we face coming into God's presence.

As it is written, "Therefore, let us come boldly to the throne of grace that we may obtain mercy and find grace to help in time of need."[508] When reading and searching through God's word, he speaks to us in written ways while he impresses upon our hearts his ways, character, and love for us and we turn to him.

Turn from Wicked Ways

Seeking God's face fills our need. It helps us turn from our wicked ways. David in his prayers asked God to "wash me completely from my iniquity, and cleanse me from my sin."[509] As David confessed his sin, he asked God to "create in me a clean heart, O God, and renew a right spirit within me,"[510] knowing he could not do it alone. David continued: "Restore to me the joy of your salvation, and uphold me a willing spirit."[511] It is not enough to just change our behavior; we need to be pleasing with the actions we take. David also wrote, "O Jehovah, open my lips, and my mouth shall show forth your praise."[512] We need to be conscious of our guilt, like David in Psalms 51:4 and 9. This constantly reminds us of God's help and place in our lives. Filled with the pollution of this world[513] and corrupted by our own sinful natures, we are helpless without God. We are unable to fill our own needs to be right with God and in good standing.[514, 515] We are normally apprehensive of the mercy given us.[516, 517] We need obedience to God's voice,[518] keeping his commandments and doing them.[519, 520, 521] This will keep us from the idols of our own creation.[522] We are to keep mercy and judgment in our lives.[523] Seeking God's face forces us to be humble before him, aligning our behavior with his as we communicate with him our lack in life through repentance.

CONCLUSION

The issues of scripture concerning Christ are a matter of prophesy. There are two forms of prophesy: the application of fulfilled prophesy and the explicitness of unfulfilled prophesy demanding attention to the details of future events. However, the infusion of our sin nature upon the relationship with God causes us to have the wage of death for the consequence of sin. This requires a fulfillment of future judgment for eternity either in the lake of fire without Christ or with Christ for eternity. Jesus Christ makes all the difference, being God in fleshly form to offer an atonement of his blood for the remission of our sins. This provides peace with God in this final judgment upon us for our sins. This peace is impossible for us because of humankind's sinfulness and inadequacy. Yet, by Christ, we have the infusion of righteousness through faith. This allows us to come to God in repentance and have circumcised hearts. For us, the only thing to finish is to participate in the sinner's prayer below by accepting Christ's atonement and his work for us as the Lamb of God through faith.

> Dear Father in Heaven,
>
> Thank you for giving us your son to come and die for our sins. Thank you for giving him as the Lamb's atonement for us and the appeasement of the judgment upon my sins. Thank you for allowing him to go to the cross to shed his blood for the remission of my sins. Thank you for raising him again on the third

day, according to the prophesy to honor your word to us, as an intercessor for me. I am a sinner, unable to meet you on your standards. Jesus, I ask you to come into my heart and live as my Savior and Lord. I accept your gift of grace and the atonement of your blood for the remission of my sins. Teach me about yourself so I can be a witness to others. Holy Spirit, I ask you to come and seal me for the day of redemption. I ask you to guide me to Christ and give me the gifts to use for the purpose of doing your will in my life. I ask the privilege of lifting Christ up in my life. I ask to live for you, Christ, all the days of my life. Father, I thank you for the grace and gift of salvation, making me one of your adopted children.

I thank you in Jesus's Name, amen.

WORKS CITED

"Dutch." (2018). Hypocrisy Sayings and Quotes. *Wise Old Sayings.* Retrieved on July 21, 2018, from http://www.wiseoldsayings.com/hypocrisy-quotes/

"Eleanor Roosevelt." (2018). Hypocrisy Sayings and Quotes. *Wise Old Sayings.* Retrieved on July 21, 2018, from http://www.wiseoldsayings.com/hypocrisy-quotes/

Holy Bible, Modern King James Version. (1998). E-Sword.

Holy Bible, New King James Version. (1982). E-Sword.

Holy Bible, Revised Version (1885). E-Sword

SomeKindaLeftist. (2017). (October 24, 2020). iFunny. Retrieved on December 6, 2024, from https://ifunny.co/picture/homosexuality-is-not-a-sin-atheism-is-not-a-sin-9XAnoqH58?s=cl

Strong, J. (1890) Strong's Hebrew and Greek Dictionaries. E-Sword

ENDNOTES

1 Matthew 5:37 NKJV
2 2 Corinthians 1:17–18 NKJV
3 Psalms 51:10–12 NKJV
4 Isaiah 57:15 NKJV
5 Luke 12:11–12 NKJV
6 John 16:8–11 NKJV
7 Hebrews 10:15 NKJV
8 1 John 5:7 NKJV
9 Isaiah 14:12–15 NKJV
10 Isaiah 12:13 NKJV
11 Isaiah 47:4 NKJV
12 Isaiah 48:12, Revelation 1:17, 2:8, 22:13 NKJV
13 Isaiah 43:15 NKJV
14 Isaiah 44:6 NKJV
15 Job 19:25–27 NKJV
16 Isaiah 46:5 NKJV
17 Romans 1:21 NKJV
18 Colossians 2:4 NKJV
19 Genesis 3:1 NKJV
20 Genesis 3:2–3 NKJV
21 Genesis 2:16–17 NKJV
22 Genesis 3:5 NKJV
23 Genesis 3:1 NKJV
24 Genesis 2:16–17 NKJV
25 Genesis 3:11 NKJV
26 1 Peter 3:7 NKJV
27 1 Corinthians 7:3 NKJV
28 1 Corinthians 14:35 NKJV
29 2 Corinthians 11:3 NKJV
30 Genesis 3:4–5 NKJV
31 Colossians 2:8 NKJV
32 Genesis 3:6 NKJV
33 James 1:15 NKJV
34 James 1:14 NKJV
35 Genesis 3:6 NKJV
36 Genesis 3:4–5 NKJV
37 Genesis 3:12–16 NKJV
38 Genesis 3:13 NKJV
39 Exodus 20:3–17 NKJV
40 Isaiah 14:12–15 NKJV
41 1 John 2:15–17 MKJV
42 1 Corinthians 11:3 MKJV
43 2 Peter 1:19–21 MKJV
44 2 Timothy 3:16–17 MKJV
45 1 Corinthians 13:33 NKJV
46 Isaiah 55:11 MKJV
47 Jeremiah 1:9–10 MKJV
48 Psalms 19 MKJV
49 Isaiah 48:3 MKJV
50 Ecclesiastes 1:11 MKJV
51 Isaiah 41:21–25 NKJV
52 Isaiah 42:9 MKJV
53 Titus 1:2 MKJV
54 Isaiah 1:18 MKJV
55 Isaiah 48:16 NKJV
56 2 Timothy 1:9 MKJV
57 Isaiah 41:4 NKJV
58 Colossians 1:16–17 NKJV
59 Zachariah 6:13 MKJV
60 Isaiah 46:10 MKJV
61 Psalms 33:10–12 MKJV

62 Isaiah 28:29 MKJV
63 Isaiah 43:10–13 MKJV
64 Psalms 119:105 MKJV
65 2 Timothy 3:16–17 MKJV
66 Jeremiah 1:12 MKJV
67 Romans 10:17 MKJV
68 Revelation 1:3 MKJV
69 Revelation 22:18–19 MKJV
70 Revelation 22:7 MKJV
71 Revelation 22:10 MKJV
72 Revelation 19:10 MKJV
73 Numbers 11:29 MKJV
74 Psalms 19:7 NKJV
75 Psalms 19:7 NKJV
76 Psalms 19:8 NKJV
77 Psalms 19:8 NKJV
78 Psalms 19:8 NKJV
79 Psalms 19:9 NKJV
80 Psalms 19:9 NKJV
81 Psalms 19:14 NKJV
82 Revelation 19:10 NKJV
83 Exodus 15:26 NKJV
84 2 Peter 1:19–21 MKJV
85 Ezekiel 37:15–17 NKJV
86 Ezekiel 37:18–20 NKJV
87 Ezekiel 37:21–28 NKJV
88 Isaiah 9:6–7 NKJV
89 Jeremiah 17:24–26 NKJV
90 Jeremiah 33:15–18 NKJV
91 Ezekiel 34:23–24 NKJV
92 Hosea 3:5 NKJV
93 Jeremiah 33:21–22 NKJV
94 Psalms 89:3 NKJV
95 Zachariah 12:8–10 NKJV
96 1 John 3:8 MKJV
97 2 Peter 2:4 NKJV
98 Jude 1:6 NKJV
99 Genesis 6:5 NKJV
100 Matthew 24:37 NKJV
101 Luke 17:26 NKJV
102 1 Peter 3:20 NKJV
103 2 Corinthians 1:10 NKJV
104 Genesis 18:20–21 NKJV
105 1 Corinthians 10:13 NKJV
106 Romans 3:10–11 NKJV
107 1 John 5:17 NKJV
108 1 John 3:4 NKJV
109 Hebrews 3:13 NKJV
110 John 8:34 MKJV
111 Hosea 4:7–8 MKJV
112 Romans 7:8–9 NKJV
113 Romans 7:14 NKJV
114 1 Corinthians 15:56 NKJV
115 Ezekiel 20:38 MKJV
116 2 Thessalonians 2:3 MKJV
117 James 1:14–15 NKJV
118 Galatians 3:20–22 NKJV
119 1 Timothy 4:2 NKJV
120 Psalms 9:16 MKJV
121 Psalms 35:8 MKJV
122 Psalms 92:7 NKJV
123 John 3:15–22 MKJV
124 Jeremiah 5:7 MKJV
125 Ezekiel 23:27 MKJV
126 Matthew 5:27 MKJV
127 Strong, H3290, "yaaqob"
128 Genesis 25:26 NKJV
129 Genesis 27:35 MKJV
130 Strong, H4820
131 Psalms 38:19 MKJV
132 Psalms 10:7 MKJV
133 Job 15:35 MKJV
134 Psalms 36:3 MKJV
135 Psalms 50:19 NKJV
136 Psalms 119:118 MKJV
137 Proverbs 12:10 MKJV
138 Proverbs 26:24 MKJV
139 Romans 6:23 MKJV
140 John 4:26 MKJV
141 Revelation 21:7–8 MKJV
142 Revelation 20:6 MKJV
143 2 Timothy 1:10 MKJV
144 Romans 10:17 NKJV
145 Hebrews 9:15 MKJV

146 Exodus 32:32–33 MKJV
147 Revelation 20:15 MKJV
148 Revelation 1:17–18 NKJV
149 Isaiah 44:6 NKJV
150 Isaiah 48:12–13 NKJV
151 Psalms 68:20 MKJV
152 2 Timothy 1:10 MKJV
153 2 Peter 2:14–16 MKJV
154 Hosea 6:6 MKJV
155 John 3:16 MKJV
156 Ezekiel 33:11 MKJV
157 Ezekiel 18:32 MKJV
158 1 Corinthians 15:26 MKJV
159 Hosea 13:14 MKJV
160 1 Corinthians 15:21–22 MKJV
161 Romans 8:6 MKJV
162 Romans 8:2 MKJV
163 Romans 6:23 MKJV
164 2 Corinthians 1:9 MKJV
165 Romans 5:17 MKJV
166 Hebrews 9:26–28 MKJV
167 Daniel 9:24 MKJV
168 Romans 9:28 MKJV
169 Revelation 21:8 MKJV
170 Hebrews 2:2–4 NKJV
171 Philippians 2:6–7 NKJV
172 Hebrews 4:15 NKJV
173 2 Corinthians 5:21 NKJV
174 Matthew 27:46 NKJV
175 Mark 15:34 NKJV
176 Isaiah 54:5 NKJV
177 Mark 8:29 NKJV
178 1 Chronicles 16:25–30 NKJV
179 John 9:38 NKJV
180 Colossians 1:15–16 NKJV
181 Genesis 2:4–7 NKJV
182 Isaiah 45:5–7 NKJV
183 Deuteronomy 4:39 NKJV
184 Deuteronomy 4:35 NKJV
185 1 Kings 8:60–61 NKJV
186 Daniel 2:23 NKJV
187 Daniel 2:47 NKJV
188 Daniel 4:34–37 NKJV
189 Genesis 2:7 NKJV
190 Isaiah 6:3 NKJV
191 Jeremiah 10:16 NKJV
192 Deuteronomy 4:24 NKJV
193 Isaiah 41:4 NKJV
194 Isaiah 44:6 NKJV
195 Revelation 22:13 NKJV
196 Genesis 2:7 MKJV
197 Isaiah 28:16 MKJV
198 John 17 NKJV
199 Isaiah 47:4 MKJV
200 Isaiah 1:18 MKJV
201 John 3:15–22 MKJV
202 Daniel 9:24 NKJV
203 Matthew 26:28 MKJV
204 Hebrews 10:17–18 MKJV
205 1 Corinthians 15:12–18 NKJV
206 Colossians 1:13 MKJV
207 Colossians 1:14 MKJV
208 Luke 1:77 MKJV
209 John 1:29 MKJV
210 Acts 5:31 MKJV
211 Hebrews 10:18–25 MKJV
212 Hebrews 8:23–28 MKJV
213 Acts 10:42–43 MKJV
214 2 Timothy 2:5–6 MKJV
215 Isaiah 7:14 MKJV
216 Luke 1:34 MKJV
217 Matthew 5:17 MKJV
218 Ephesians 3:9–11 MKJV
219 Hebrews 12:2 MKJV
220 Isaiah 46:9–10 MKJV
221 Ephesians 1:10–11 MKJV
222 1 John 3:8 NKJV
223 Romans 8:28 MKJV
224 Isaiah 29:15 MKJV
225 2 Timothy 4:1 MKJV
226 Hebrews 9:27 MKJV
227 Revelation 20:13 MKJV
228 2 Corinthians 5:10 MKJV
229 Revelation 20:12 MKJV

230 Exodus 32:32–33 MKJV
231 Revelation 20:15 MKJV
232 2 Samuel 22:6 MKJV
233 Luke 16:22–26 MKJV
234 Revelation 20:14 MKJV
235 Revelation 1:17–18 MKJV
236 Isaiah 5:14, 16 MKJV
237 Isaiah 14:15 MKJV
238 Jude 1:6 MKJV
239 Matthew 10:28 MKJV
240 James 3:6 MKJV
241 Matthew 23:15 NKJV
242 James 3:8 NKJV
243 Proverbs 12:15 NKJV
244 Jeremiah 17:9 MKJV
245 Job 10:1 MKJV
246 Proverbs 19:21 MKJV
247 Genesis 6:5 MKJV
248 Genesis 8:21 MKJV
249 Titus 3:9–11 NKJV
250 Romans 2:8 NKJV
251 Job 32:1–2 NKJV
252 Colossians 2:23 NKJV
253 Ecclesiastes 8:5 NKJV
254 Romans 8:3 NKJV
255 Mark 9:38 NKJV
256 Romans 7:12–13 NKJV
257 2 Timothy 3:1–5 NKJV
258 Strong, G1467, "egkrateuomai"
259 Strong, G1466, "egkraeia"
260 Strong, G5367, "philautos"
261 Strong, G846, "autos"
262 Strong, G5384, "philos"
263 John 12:25 NKJV
264 Hebrews 13:5 MKJV
265 1 Timothy 6:10 MKJV
266 Isaiah 55:1 NKJV
267 Matthew 5:6 NKJV
268 Revelation 7:16–17 NKJV
269 Isaiah 14:11–15 NKJV
270 James 4:16 MKJV
271 Job 32:1–2 NKJV
272 Romans 2:23 NKJV
273 2 Corinthians 12:6 NKJV
274 Ephesians 2:9–10 MKJV
275 2 Samuel 17:28 MKJV
276 Psalms 73:6 MKJV
277 Proverbs 11:2 MKJV
278 1 John 2:16 MKJV
279 Obadiah 1:3 MKJV
280 Job 9:13 MKJV
281 Job 28:8 MKJV
282 Psalms 31:20 MKJV
283 Job 35:20 MKJV
284 Proverbs 16:18 MKJV
285 Proverbs 8:13 MKJV
286 Luke 12:10 MKJV
287 Mark 3:19–29 MKJV
288 Matthew 12:31 MKJV
289 2 Samuel 12:14 MKJV
290 Romans 1:25 MKJV
291 Revelation 2:9 MKJV
292 Revelation 13:6 MKJV
293 Ephesians 2:1–2 NKJV
294 Ephesians 3:6 MKJV
295 Colossians 3:5–7 MKJV
296 Hebrews 2:3 MKJV
297 Luke 6:35 MKJV
298 1 Chronicles 16:34 NKJV
299 Romans 1:21 NKJV
300 Colossians 3:17 NKJV
301 Hebrews 13:15 NKJV
302 Psalms 30:4 NKJV
303 Psalms 87:12 NKJV
304 Psalms 100:1–5 NKJV
305 Colossians 3:14–15 NKJV
306 Isaiah 32:17–18 NKJV
307 Revelation 11:17 NKJV
308 Daniel 6:10 NKJV
309 Hebrews 10:29 MKJV
310 Leviticus 10:10 MKJV
311 Deuteronomy 12:8 MKJV
312 Judges 21:25 MKJV
313 Job 31:1 MKJV

314 Proverbs 3:7 MKJV
315 Proverbs 16:2 MKJV
316 Proverbs 21:2 MKJV
317 Isaiah 5:21 MKJV
318 1 Timothy 1:8–10 MKJV
319 Romans 1:21 MKJV
320 Romans 1:22–23 MKJV
321 Romans 1:24 MKJV
322 Genesis 6:5 MKJV
323 Ezra 2:4 MKJV
324 Romans 1:26–27 MKJV
325 Romans 1:24–25 NKJV
326 Leviticus 18:22 NKJV
327 Exodus 7:14 MKJV
328 Exodus 9:12 MKJV
329 Exodus 9:34 MKJV
330 Matthew 23:15 MKJV
331 Deuteronomy 10:16 NKJV
332 Deuteronomy 11:16 MKJV
333 Deuteronomy 30:17 MKJV
334 Deuteronomy 30:6 MKJV
335 Hebrews 4:12 MKJV
336 Exodus 20:16 MKJV
337 Exodus 23:1 MKJV
338 Proverbs 12:17 MKJV
339 Deuteronomy 19:16–17 MKJV
340 2 Peter 2:12–16 MKJV
341 Galatians 5:22 NKJV
342 2 Peter 1:5–7 MKJV
343 Genesis 49:7 MKJV
344 Genesis 6:11 MKJV
345 Genesis 49:5 MKJV
346 Psalms 55:9 MKJV
347 MKJV
348 Jeremiah 20:8 MKJV
349 Zephaniah 3:4 MKJV
350 Habakkuk 1:3 MKJV
351 Romans 8:28 NKJV
352 Psalms 119:158 MKJV
353 Proverbs 11:3 MKJV
354 Revelation 3:17 NKJV
355 Proverbs 13:15 MKJV
356 Hosea 6:7 MKJV
357 Ecclesiastes 3:18 MKJV
358 Judges 9:4 MKJV
359 Romans 10:17 MKJV
360 1 Timothy 3:5 NKJV
361 Hebrews 1:1 NKJV
362 Exodus 5:9 MKJV
363 Exodus 20:7 MKJV
364 Job 11:11 MKJV
365 Psalms 39:6 MKJV
366 Psalms 73:10 MKJV
367 Psalms 127:1 MKJV
368 Isaiah 45:19 MKJV
369 Matthew 15:9 MKJV
370 Colossians 2:8 MKJV
371 Titus 3:9 MKJV
372 Leviticus 26:19 MKJV
373 1 Samuel 17:28 MKJV
374 2 Chronicles 32:26 MKJV
375 Job 9:13 NKJV
376 Obadiah 1:3 MKJV
377 Jeremiah 17:9 NKJV
378 Psalms 10:4 MKJV
379 Proverbs 8:13 MKJV
380 Malachi 1:10 MKJV
381 Philippians 2:13 MKJV
382 Hebrews 10:38 MKJV
383 Habakkuk 2:4 MKJV
384 2 Peter 2:12–15 MKJV
385 Proverbs 11:9 MKJV
386 Colossians 2:4 MKJV
387 James 1:8 MKJV
388 James 4:8 MKJV
389 Acts 17:11 MKJV
390 Psalms 12:2 MKJV
391 Matthew 7:5 MKJV
392 James 4:12 NKJV
393 Matthew 23:15 MKJV
394 Hebrews 1:1 MKJV
395 Habakkuk 2:4 MKJV
396 Hebrews 11:6 MKJV
397 Hebrews 12:1–2 MKJV

398 Hebrews 11:13–16 MKJV
399 Hebrews 11:33 MKJV
400 1 Kings 17:1–24 NKJV
401 Hebrews 12:1 MKJV
402 Hebrews 11:39–40 MKJV
403 Hebrews 11:51 MKJV
404 Genesis 4:4 MKJV
405 Hebrews 11:51 MKJV
406 Hebrews 11:4 MKJV
407 Hebrews 12:22–24 MKJV
408 Romans 5:16–17 MKJV
409 1 Kings 8:39 MKJV
410 Hebrews 12:2 MKJV
411 Job 31:33 MKJV
412 Hebrews 7:11–28 MKJV
413 Hosea 6:6 NKJV
414 Hosea 6:6–7 MKJV
415 John 15:7 MKJV
416 Genesis 5:22 MKJV
417 Hebrews 11:5 MKJV
418 Revelation 11:4–10 NKJV
419 Jude 14–15 MKJV
420 Genesis 6:8–9 MKJV
421 James 2:17–18 MKJV
422 Genesis 6:8–9 MKJV
423 Hebrews 11:7 MKJV
424 2 Peter 2:5 MKJV
425 Genesis 6:22 MKJV
426 Genesis 5:29 MKJV
427 Ezekiel 14:14, 20 MKJV
428 Genesis 7:1 MKJV
429 1 Peter 3:18–22 MKJV
430 Romans 4:3 MKJV
431 Genesis 22:8 RV
432 Romans 4:11 NKJV
433 Romans 4:3–5 MKJV
434 Hebrews 11:8–10 MKJV
435 Hebrews 11:17 MKJV
436 Acts 2:38 NKJV
437 Acts 3:19 MKJV
438 Luke 23:42 MKJV
439 Luke 23:43 NKJV
440 Romans 10:8–11 NKJV
441 Romans 6:23 MKJV
442 Romans 3:23 MKJV
443 Romans 3:10–11 MKJV
444 Galatians 2:21 MKJV
445 Romans 10:4 NKJV
446 Hebrews 4:12 NKJV
447 2 Timothy 3:16–17 MKJV
448 James 1:20 MKJV
449 1 John 3:10 MKJV
450 Philippians 3:9 MKJV
451 1 Corinthians 1:30–31 MKJV
452 Romans 10:9–10 MKJV
453 Titus 3:4–7 MKJV
454 1 Peter 3:14–16 MKJV
455 Psalms 19 NKJV
456 Deuteronomy 10:16–17 MKJV
457 Deuteronomy 30:6 MKJV
458 Jeremiah 4:4 MKJV
459 Jeremiah 9:24 MKJV
460 Matthew 3:8 MKJV
461 Matthew 9:13 MKJV
462 Mark 2:17 MKJV
463 Luke 24:46–47 MKJV
464 2 Peter 3:9 MKJV
465 Romans 12:2 MKJV
466 2 Corinthians 7:10 MKJV
467 Mark 1:4 MKJV
468 Acts 5:31–32 MKJV
469 John 3:15–17 MKJV
470 2 Chronicles 7:14 MKJV
471 Leviticus 23:32 MKJV
472 Ezra 8:21 MKJV
473 Psalms 10:17 MKJV
474 Isaiah 57:15 MKJV
475 Matthew 18:4 MKJV
476 James 4:6 MKJV
477 Hebrews 4:16 MKJV
478 Hebrews 1:1 ESV+
479 Genesis 3:8 NKJV
480 2 Timothy 3:16–17
481 1 John 4:1–3 NKJV

482 2 Thessalonians 5:21 ESV+
483 2 Corinthians 13:5 ESV+
484 Job 22:27 KJV
485 Revelation 3:18 NKJV
486 Psalms 64:1 MKJV
487 Deuteronomy 6:24 MKJV
488 John 15:7 MKJV
489 Psalms 61:7 ESV+
490 Psalms 86:2 MKJV
491 Isaiah 49:8–10 MKJV
492 Matthew 6:8 MKJV
493 Psalms 69:13 MKJV
494 Revelation 7:10 MKJV
495 Hebrews 2:3 MKJV
496 Psalms 60:20 MKJV
497 Daniel 9:13 MKJV
498 Romans 12:12–15 MKJV
499 1 Corinthians 7:5 MKJV
500 Colossian 4:2–4 MKJV
501 Nehemiah 1:6–11 MKJV
502 James 5:15–16 MKJV
503 Hebrews 11:6 MKJV
504 Matthew 6:33 MKJV
505 Luke 12:31 MKJV
506 John 5:30 MKJV
507 Zechariah 2:11 MKJV
508 Hebrews 4:16 MKJV
509 Psalms 51:2 MKJV
510 Psalms 51:10 MKJV
511 Psalms 51:12 MKJV
512 Psalms 51:15 MKJV
513 Psalms 51:5, 7, 10 MKJV
514 Psalms 51:11 MKJV
515 Psalms 109:21–22 MKJV
516 Psalms 51:1 MKJV
517 Psalms 130:4 MKJV
518 Deuteronomy 4:30 MKJV
519 Nehemiah 1:9 MKJV
520 John 14:15, 21 MKJV
521 John 15:10 MKJV
522 Ezekiel 14:6 MKJV
523 Hosea 12:6 MKJV

ABOUT THE AUTHOR

Jay T. Attebery AACS, BSTM, MNCM, MISM earned four degrees and is a retired prodigal son who considers himself a lay human. He enjoys studying the Bible and clarifying the hard things in Scripture and doctrine. A survivor of sexual abuse and a recovered alcoholic, he has been sober for more than forty years and is living a life of compassion, repentance, and forgiveness.

Made in the USA
Columbia, SC
05 July 2025

71bc27ba-ca3a-4340-bfac-0a39925aeb28R01